THE FIBERARTS
BOOK OF
WEARABLE ART

THE FIBERARTS
BOOK OF
WEARABLE ART

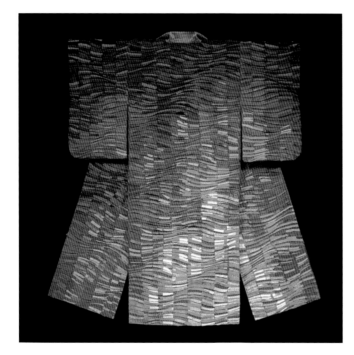

Katherine Duncan Aimone

LARK BOOKS

A Division of Sterling Publishing Co., Inc.
New York

Acknowledgments

THANKS TO:

- Rob Pulleyn, Carol Taylor, and Deborah Morgenthal for giving me this wonderful book assignment.

- Sunita Patterson, editor of *FIBERARTS*, for serving as a willing sounding board throughout the process of writing the book.

- Ann Batchelder, former editor of *FIBERARTS*, for lending ideas during the initial stages of planning the book.

- Matt Chambers, Rickie Wesbrooks, and other staff members at Bellagio in Asheville, North Carolina, for their assistance and encouragement during the research stage of the book.

- All of the artists who answered my seemingly endless streams of e-mails and phone calls during their busy days. Thanks also for the encouragement of a few who went beyond the call of duty (you know who you are).

- My husband, Steve Aimone, who listened very patiently to my first drafts and provided comments that made the book a better one.

- Veronica Gunther for her assistance throughout the process of creating the book.

- Dana Irwin—last but certainly not least—for creating a gorgeous, sophisticated layout that does justice to the work of the artists.

Art Director: DANA IRWIN

Cover Design: BARBARA ZARETSKY

Assistant Art Director: HANNES CHAREN,

Production Assistance: MEGAN KIRBY,

SHANNON YOKELEY

Editorial Assistance:

VERONIKA ALICE GUNTER,

RAIN NEWCOMB, HEATHER SMITH

Editorial Interns:

ANNE WOLFF HOLLYFIELD,

NATHALIE MORNU

Cover:

Mike Kane and Steve Sells, *Woodgrain Blocks Kimono*, 2001; silk chiffon; arashi shibori discharge, itajimi discharge dyed.

Photo: John F. Cooper. Model: Julie Zeger

Page 3:

Tim Harding, *Gold Wave Kimono*, 1999; silk; stitched, cut, pressed.

Photo: Petronella Ytsma

Page 6:

Carter Smith, *Secrets* (K dresses); 2000; silk and rayon, black cut satin; shibori pattern.

Photo: Joan Emm

Dedication

This book is dedicated to my parents—Margaret Flexer Duncan and Pope Alexander Duncan—both remarkably kind and talented people.

Library of Congress Cataloging-in-Publication Data

Duncan-Aimone, Katherine.
   The fiberarts book of wearable art / by Katherine Duncan Aimone.
      p. cm.
   ISBN 1-57990-515-3
   1. Clothing and dress. 2. Textile crafts. 3. Wearable art. I. Title.

TT560 .D86 2002
746--dc21

2001050585

10 9 8 7 6 5 4 3 2 1

Published by Lark Books, a division of
Sterling Publishing Co., Inc.
387 Park Avenue South, New York, N.Y. 10016

First Paperback Edition 2003
© 2002, Lark Books

Distributed in Canada by Sterling Publishing,
c/o Canadian Manda Group, One Atlantic Ave., Suite 105
Toronto, Ontario, Canada M6K 3E7

Distributed in the U.K. by:
Guild of Master Craftsman Publications Ltd.
Castle Place 166 High Street, Lewes, East Sussex
England BN7 1XU
Tel: (+ 44) 1273 477374
Fax: (+ 44) 1273 478606
Email: pubs@thegmcgroup.com
Web: www.gmcpublications.com

Distributed in Australia by Capricorn Link (Australia) Pty Ltd., P.O. Box 704, Windsor, NSW 2756 Australia

The written instructions, photographs, designs, patterns, and projects in this volume are intended for the personal use of the reader and may be reproduced for that purpose only. Any other use, especially commercial use, is forbidden under law without written permission of the copyright holder.

Every effort has been made to ensure that all the information in this book is accurate. However, due to differing conditions, tools, and individual skills, the publisher cannot be responsible for any injuries, losses, and other damages that may result from the use of the information in this book.

If you have questions or comments about this book, please contact:
Lark Books
67 Broadway
Asheville, NC 28801
(828) 253-0467

Printed in China

ISBN 1-57990-515-3

CONTENTS

If you've ever acquired a piece of artwear, you probably first felt drawn to its color and texture, connected with it through touch, and gazed in amazement at the transformation that occurred as you put it on. These beautiful works of art resonate with the creative thought of the maker, and magically, the wearer becomes a part of that energy. These are pieces that are often kept for a lifetime by collectors—who wear them again and again to experience their beauty and complexity.

This book explores the compelling work of 39 of the most fertile minds in the field of

INTRODUCTION

wearable art (or art-to-wear). Their thoughts and personal stories are as inspiring as their work. Many of them have backgrounds in traditional fields of fine art, and at some point in their careers, segued into making art-to-wear in response to a variety of ambitions. Every one is an artist, whether they call themselves a designer, a maker of art clothing, or any other descriptor.

A lot of them talk about their need to "run their own show" and live an independent and meaningful life outside of the corporate mainstream. Because of this choice, they constantly juggle their time between making and marketing their work and experimenting with new ideas. Some make only one-of-a-kind pieces, others create both one-of-a-kind and limited edition pieces. A few orchestrate and make collections by collaborating with fellow artists. But all of them hold fast to their inclination to be in charge of the process from inception to creation, rather than work as designers whose concepts are determined by a changing fashion market. Most of these artists are blatantly unwilling to sacrifice their ethical standards about how the work is made and the manner in which it is put out into the world.

For close to 30 years, *FIBERARTS* magazine has honored the work of textile artists who make clothing. Even as this book is being prepared for print, new work is emerging in the field of wearable art. Sadly, we were not able to present every talented American artist that creates art-to-wear, but sought to give an overview of the field and its many techniques and approaches.

On the following pages, you'll read essays written by two well-known artists who have been involved in the American wearable art movement since its inception. Tim Harding presents a distilled and very helpful chronology and the cultural context from which the movement sprang. Susan Summa writes about art-to-wear from the perspective of one who has been passionately engaged in it as a lifestyle.

Clothing as an art form is more relevant today than ever. The availability of mass-produced products in our world, where change happens in the blink of an eye, makes us to long for things that are more personal and timeless. Art-to-wear offers us the opportunity to experience works that perfectly merge artistic and functional intention, as the images that follow so beautifully illustrate.

THE ART-TO-WEAR MOVEMENT IN AMERICA

BY TIM HARDING

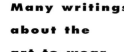

Many writings about the art-to-wear movement in the United States have accurately related it to the political and social climate in the late 1960s and early 1970s. Alternatives to the mainstream culture developed across many facets of American life. Personal freedom and antiwar sentiments were hallmarks of the new counterculture. As a part of a new freedom of expression, personal adornment and dress were influenced by ethnic clothing, feminism, and an antifashion and antiestablishment mood. Not yet considered an art form, this alternative dress was loosely called "body art."

art-to-wear. The new movement attracted weavers, quilters, knitters, painters, costumers, dyers, and other artists interested in experimenting with the intrinsic physical properties of fibers and fabrics in relationship to the body. These artists often combined traditional techniques and materials with new ones.

This populist movement began in opposition to a rigid fine art hierarchy that relegated craft to the lowest level of its ranks. Fiber was considered to be of the least importance within the craft field, and fiber wearables—traditionally considered as "women's work"—were not taken seriously at all. For the growing countermovement, the Japanese kimono became emblematic of an object's potential to effectively fuse aesthetic and functional concerns.

As art school students began to embrace the expressive potential of the human form through body art, a small movement grew spontaneously within the larger, more established Studio Craft Movement (a movement that emerged shortly after World War II in the art departments of American universities). Interest in the art object as both aesthetic and functional acted as a common bond between these movements. New York and San Francisco became geographic centers for

Members of this movement held a strong conviction that a successful piece of wearable art could be as legitimate a form of artistic expression as a painting. They also believed that the art hierarchy of Western culture had historically maintained significant social barriers between art and life. Art should not be relegated to elite temples of culture, such as museums, but should be an intimate part of everyday life and intimate as garments.

Ellen Marsh and Robin McKay, *Red Bird (Transparencies Collection)*, 2000; silk organza; discharge paste printed; black georgette silk tank dress.
Photo: Wit McKay

In painting, the viewer must look through the window established by the picture plane in order to experience the artist's vision. Artists who created art-to-wear pondered the relevance of this approach with questions such as: Can the artist break that barrier and involve the viewer in the creative act? Can the viewer be directly involved in the work?

The creation of art in the form of a garment could allow a viewer to step into a piece to feel its weight and its texture. Many art-to-wear artists consider the piece incomplete without its final stage in which the viewer animates the piece by wearing it. The art-to-wear movement had no manifesto, but its early pioneers and innovators widely held these premises, forming a conceptual foundation for a new art form.

By the mid-1970s, the American Craft Council began to create a national marketplace for the Studio Craft Movement through a series of annual craft fairs that included art-to-wear. These fairs brought together the artists, galleries, and shops as well as the movement's early and all-important collectors. As a result, the movement grew and flourished. Many other fairs cropped up that emulated the American Craft Council model, notably a handful of high-quality museum-sponsored events.

In 1983, the American Craft Museum in New York mounted an exhibition entitled *Art to Wear: New Handmade Clothing* that toured nine states and traveled the following year to many Southeast Asian venues. This event, more than any other single show, finally lent legitimacy to a movement that was more than a decade old. Other museums mounted shows, and some began collections of art-to-wear. American magazines such as *American Craft*, *FIBERARTS*, and *Ornament* published articles about the movement and specific artists.

With this greater exposure, the movement progressed during the 1980s and became commercially successful. It received added attention as it began to have an influence on the fashion industry. The resulting growth stemmed in part from the movement's new accessibility to mainstream culture. Whether this acceptance signaled maturation of the movement or a compromising of ideals is debatable. The movement changed along with the culture. As a result, it became more mainstream and watered down. The raw energy of its early days dissipated, and a lot of work became derivative imitations of innovators' work. Even handpainted T-shirts took on the designation of wearable art.

During the late 1980s and early 1990s, a significant turnover of talent occurred. Some of the initial innovators moved on to other pursuits, while others continued and evolved. The once rebellious, young, populist artists now had children and financial concerns such as mortgages to consider; thus they engaged a more pragmatic perspective. New people joined the movement with a stronger emphasis on design than on art and craft. Through a slow and continuous evolution, the early and cumbersome forms of art-to-wear became refined. With improved craftsmanship and detail, they emphasized comfort, fit, drape, and fluidity.

The cover of the *FIBERARTS* (January/February 1998) featuring the work of Susan Summa.

Today, one might say that the now-fragmented movement is larger, much more diverse, and more closely associated with fashion than art. It numbers more artist/designers, more craft fairs, more retailers, and more collectors. The new work synthesizes early inspirations, the new marketplace, fashion, the craft world, the art world, pop culture, and the current social and political climate. To many creators of art-to-wear, it matters little whether their work is labeled as fine art, decorative art, or applied art, as long as they are able to pursue their vision and form of expression. The ongoing democratization of fashion, the melding of highbrow and lowbrow culture, and the cross-fertilization of previously distinct fields have all influenced the popularization of art-to-wear. In some ways, the goals of the early populist movement have been realized.

The ongoing challenge for the art-to-wear movement is to reinvigorate itself. It is hoped that a new generation will continue to create work out of equally high ideals. As new materials and technologies trickle down from industry, artists will no doubt adapt them for personal expression. Already, high-tech fibers and techniques such as bonding, heat transfer, and new variations of reactive-chemical surface design and structure collapse have gained importance in the field.

Currently, the most serious edge of the movement continues to evolve, experiment, and explore. Its participants continue to create innovative—perhaps less strikingly expressive but more beautifully functional and subtle—garments that are fed by the movement's conceptual foundations.

Harding is a working artist who has been actively involved in the art-to-wear movement.

A PERSONAL LOOK AT AN EVOLVING MOVEMENT

BY SUSAN SUMMA

Not one of us owns a crystal ball. Few of us have the foresight in our youth to see what we will make of our lives. We have no clue of how we may influence the world. Some of us choose a path without knowing where it will lead us. Sometimes, this is an advantage.

I wear the colorful coat of an artist, a creator, and a rebel. During the mid-1960s, I inadvertently became part of a small group of gifted, instinctive, and committed pioneering artists. We didn't know then what a fascinating and sometimes difficult life was in store for us. We had no idea of the evocative and collective creative force we would manifest. And we certainly didn't know that the garments we were beginning to produce in our studios and spare rooms were to become the basis of a new movement in American art and fashion.

My own evolving definition of the wearable art movement comes out of the years of experiencing the process of making cloth as well as a gratifying exchange between artists and close friends in the field for more than three decades. The movement has been such an integral part of my life, the need to create and sell so necessary to my survival, and the drive to continue to grow and explore so intrinsic to my curiosity, that I've rarely stopped to examine the bigger picture. Those of us who spend our days in our studios—dreaming of color, pattern, and texture before engineering the work to reflect our thinking—live an inward life. Only on the rare occasions when we emerge from our studios to sell, travel, teach, or be taught do we connect with our peers, our collectors, our students, and our galleries.

I, like many of my colleagues, was encouraged as a child to explore my artistic side. Many of us were also lucky enough to learn a variety of needle arts from our

Left:
Arlene Wohl at her loom in her studio.

grandmothers, great aunts, and mothers. As we came of age in the mid-1960s and attended colleges across the country, we were surrounded by an array of colorful clothing—such as embroidered jeans, skirts made from East Indian fabrics, Moroccan vests, and Chinese hats. Fabrics from all over the world were finding their way onto the surfaces of our clothes. The word "ethnic" suddenly became part of our daily vocabulary, and we were eager to shed our polyester blends and nylon pantyhose for "real" fabrics! The political climate of the 1960s and early 1970s set the stage for some major rebellion—in essence, we didn't want to act like the previous generation, and we certainly didn't want to look like them! We experimented with tie dye, bead

Jean Cacicedo dyeing cloth in her studio.

stringing, textural crochet, and knitting. Those of us who were lucky enough to find a loom learned to weave.

Soon, friends wanted to buy our artwear. Craft fairs sprang up. Classes were taught. We bought books by the dozens, shared ideas, and began traveling across the country to meet and to sell our work. Gallery owners took the risk of purchasing our wild creations, and their loyal patrons rewarded them by buying our work. The fledgling world of wearable art, artwear, or art-to-wear (as it also came to be called) was wide-open.

There were no rules, and the creativity of each garment was far more valued than fit, fashion, or construction detail and quality.

As the 1970s progressed, fiber art found its way into every region of the country. Craft shows on the east and west coasts of the United States were meccas for artists and collectors, providing an ideal environment for meeting other artists experimenting in textiles and for sharing our passion with collectors. Our proximity to and friendships with craftsmen making other art forms also served as inspiration. The encouragement of collectors and galleries led us to new creative heights and served as an ongoing source of emotional and financial support. In turn, the collectors who chose our work fed their own search for individualism. For those of us creating garments full time, these shows provided a primary source of income as well as support, education, and socialization. On a creative high after shows, filled with new ideas and enthusiasm, we would return to the solitude of our studios. The circuslike lifestyle was intense, exhilarating, and often exhausting!

As artwear became more popular and a demand for it grew, gallery owners flocked to the shows to purchase our work in increasing quantities. Suddenly we were faced with an unexpected and heady dilemma: how to make more, make it faster, and accomplish this without losing our originality and creativity. Heated questions about the ethics of wearable work resulted, such as: Could a garment be designated as "handmade" if any piece of machinery was involved? Could adding just one more set of helping hands destroy the spirit of the garment? How big could a studio be before it should be called a manufacturing plant?

Changes in our marketplace were reflected by the growing demand by patrons to make pieces that fit! Not everyone wanted to collect garments that were shapeless and voluminous body-canvases. Our collectors and galleries began asking for sized garments instead of accepting the one-size-fits-many concept. During the

1990s, as the marketplace for artwear became increasingly savvy, many galleries also began requesting colors that more closely followed fashion trends, more sophisticated silhouettes, finer finishing details and construction, and more refined embellishment. The movement was growing up, and for many of us this was not an entirely welcome change!

The artwear designers who embraced this change developed an awareness that the creative spirit had to be blended with business acumen. In those days, it was rare to find a designer with a business background, but to be successful it became crucial to know about business, marketing, and management. It was also critical to remain highly creative and productive. While our mainstream friends had been earning their M.B.A.'s, we had been learning our art. The struggling lifestyle that had once seemed romantic—driving overloaded, old vans across the country to attend craft shows and raising organic gardens to feed ourselves—became outdated. Now it was time for us to pull ourselves up by our entrepreneurial bootstraps and speed-learn the business of art.

Many of us began to question our choices. None of us regretted our decisions to make art, but we entered a period of reevaluation. Some no longer wanted to make production work and began to make one-of-a-kind work again. Some decided to teach in order to be able to experiment with new techniques and nurture the next generation of fiber designers. Some chose to move further into creation of well-designed, fashion-oriented collections. This book represents many of those who chose to move forward with unique works as well as those who decided to bridge the gap with collections inspired by their best creative visions.

This latter group of studio designers began to have a strong impact on the fashion market. During the later 1970s and 1980s, many large manufacturers began producing garments closely inspired by unique artwear garments. Commercial sweaters began to mimic graphic art knits, and commercial cloth began to draw inspiration from handwoven textiles. Competition from industry became a major market force, prompting us to forge new territory. Even though this change seemed to be natural in the evolution of artwear as a business, this new competition posed a major challenge for those of us selling in the larger marketplace.

As I look back over 30 years in the artwear world, I see a critically important collaboration between the artists, the collectors, the gallery owners, and the media. Without all four of these interlocking elements in place,

Jorie Johnson piecing and manipulating wool to create felted pieces.

Ana Lisa Hedstrom, Untitled, 2001; fabric for three-piece dress printed with computer-generated image of dyed fabric; dye sublimation transfer printing.
Printing: Alyson LeBlanc
Photo: Kim Harrington

the movement might have faltered shortly after the point of its inception. Without the gallery owners who took a risk in purchasing our early work and continued to buy from us, we wouldn't have been able to survive financially. The galleries also gave us critical feedback from their clients that helped us to stretch and grow.

The most influential galleries in the category of artwear over the years have been Julie: Artisans' Gallery, New York City, New York; Santa Fe Weaving Gallery, Santa Fe, New Mexico; Obiko, San Francisco, California (now gone); and Jacqueline Lippitz Gallery Art to Wear in Glencoe, Illinois (now gone). Within a few years, a second generation of galleries supporting artwear was established; including Dream Weaver in Sarasota, Florida, and Martha's Vineyard, Massachusetts; Northern Possessions in Chicago, Illinois; Turtledove in Philadelphia, Pennsylvania; Bazaar Del Mundo in San Diego, California; Jackie Chalkley in Washington, D.C.; and Bellagio in Asheville, North Carolina.

In many instances, these galleries made financial sacrifices in order to represent a wide variety of artists on an ongoing basis, and it was their passion that drove the market for our creations. In turn, these galleries' clients became our collectors, creating a broader market for our work by wearing it where it would receive attention.

What will come forth as we move into another century? For artwear designers at the creative edge today, new techniques and new fibers are a focal point. From digital printing, to heat-set sculpting of synthetic fabric, to creating textures by combining and manipulating fibers with surface chemicals...new and exciting horizons are ahead. The artistry of artwear comes not from the materials, techniques, or machinery, but from the intention of the artist using them. Art-to-wear has continued to derive its impetus from an immense curiosity and an explicit rebellion against the accepted order of the day.

Today's definition of art-to-wear stems from elements inherent to both art and costume: the drape of the cloth, the way the cloth moves with the body, attention to fine craftsmanship, line, proportion, scale, composition, color, and texture. Setting it apart from costume is the added dimension of dramatic personal statement in narrative graphic, in word, or in implied message that expresses each artist's unique voice. Art-to-wear is the external expression of deeply held personal identity as well as the unique fusion between the artist's intense personal vision and the collector's response.

Through change and challenge, new visions for the movement will be given a voice. The next version of it lies ahead, and the creators shouldn't be imprisoned by tradition. Artwear will continue to surprise and delight the wearers of the future. Those of us who considered ourselves to be visionary risk-takers and bohemians should be the first to herald change! What an intriguing world for artwear will continue to evolve as artistic vision and technological innovation are applied to space wear, smart clothing, and more.

Summa is the founder of Atelier, an exclusive New York show of artwear for the wholesale trade that is held three times yearly.

THE ARTISTS

ANA LISA HEDSTROM

EMERYVILLE, CALIFORNIA

"I OFTEN REFER TO SHIBORI AS A LANGUAGE. THE PATTERNS, WHETHER THEY RESULT FROM STITCHING, FOLDING, AND CLAMPING, OR WRAPPING ON A TUBE, KEEP THE IMPRINT OF THIS PHYSICAL ACTION. I THINK THERE IS A CEREBRAL PLEASURE FOR THE VIEWER TO FOLLOW A CHANGING PATTERN. PERHAPS THIS IS THE KEY TO THE ENDURING APPEAL OF COMPRESSION-RESIST DYED FABRIC...THROUGH TIME, CULTURES, GENDER, AND AGE."

Opposite page:
Ana Lisa Hedstrom, *Coat*, 1998; silk; resist dyed, pieced.
Photo: Kevin Meynal

Above:
Ana Lisa Hedstrom, Untitled, 1999; shibori resist-dyed skirts and scarves, silk sweaters dyed by Bettina Zurek.
Photo: Jeff Novick

Right:
Ana Lisa Hedstrom, *Tunic, Skirt, and Scarf*, 1979; silk; shibori, pleated.
Photo: Craig Morey

of New York department stores, finding high-quality seamstresses, and meeting deadlines.

Today, she thinks of her studio as a lab for testing new ideas and applications. For years her signature has been the patterning and piecing of one-of-a-kind silk coats created with the same eye for juxtapositions as that of a collage artist. A process-oriented, intuitive approach has fed her fascination for the possibilities of surface design on silk. Perhaps that is why her current work looks as fresh and new as ever.

The innate tension of opposites fuels her imagination as she searches for the "surprising or unlikely" in her work. If this excitement is missing in her work, it doesn't feel complete to her. She recognizes the necessity of some anxiety and doubt that accompany the creation of satisfying work.

She thinks of music as a correlation for her work in terms of color and composition, and is comfortable with the open-ended nature of working in the abstract. Like a musician, she'll often choose a compositional theme and work on it until she "exhausts" the subject. When the period of exploration and discovery ends, she moves on to another theme.

Although Ana Lisa Hedstrom once noted that she doesn't consider her work to be "really important," she has nevertheless been a constant figure in the art-to-wear movement and an inspiration for many second-generation artists who make clothing.

She acknowledges that in the heady, early days of art-to-wear, her work, like those of others, was a "rebellious impulse to break the established conventions of dress." She reflects that "in all rebellions the subversive evaporates quickly, and, in our case, the commercial became a part of the movement."

Nevertheless, Hedstrom has been primarily motivated by the experimental, evolving nature of her work while never completely embracing a business context for it. In the early 1990s, she became frustrated with the production aspects of making clothing for a high-end market, including conforming to the fashion calendar

An acknowledged master dyer and colorist (and a teacher in this field), she notes color as the primary impetus in her work and has used the processes of arashi shibori resist-dyeing, overdyeing, airbrushing, and painting to create her designs on fabric. She often tacks pieces of prepared or partially prepared silk to the walls of her studio and allows her subconscious to work on the best placement of pieces in the construction of the garment. In reality, this often means trips back and forth to the dye pot to alter this or that.

Like many artists who make clothing, she is a painter first and a garment-maker second. Today, she is producing large wall works for interiors. For her, it's all the same process—clothing and pieces for hanging—and one idea plays off another.

Her newer clothing is less dependent on the detailed sewing that she undertook in the past, or even the fine fabrics. For instance, she is combining cotton cheesecloth and polyester chiffon to make cloqué jackets or using devoré to distress linen/silk to produce a "shaggy" layer bonded to gauze. She has found a new enthusiasm for using shibori techniques to resist-scour crepe silk imported from Japan, creating areas of stiff and soft silk that take the dye differently.

She is also experimenting with computer-generated designs. She uses the computer to scan the patterns of her fabric swatches before she modifies them with a photo program. This expands her possibilities of design tremendously, and she has the fabric printed for clothing through the process of a dye sublimation transfer printing process. She sees this approach and technology as a large part of her future. Nonetheless, she is still drawn to the "hands-on dialogue of working with cloth, string, PVC pipe, and a dye pot"——what she affectionately calls the "mundane tools to produce engaging and irresistible patterns and texture on cloth."

Opposite page:
Ana Lisa Hedstrom, *Coat*, 1998; silk pique; resist dyed, pieced.
Photo: Kevin Meynal

Left:
Ana Lisa Hedstrom, *Tunic*, 2001; polyester; computer-manipulated dye sublimation print from scanned shibori scrap.

Above:
Ana Lisa Hedstrom, Untitled, 2000; silk pique; resist dyed and pieced.
Photo: Jeff Novick

ELLEN & ROBIN
MARSH & MCKAY

OAKLAND, CALIFORNIA & NEW YORK, NEW YORK

"THE SYMBOLS I USE IN MY IMAGES ARE TAKEN FROM MANY DIFFERENT CULTURES AND SIMPLE SHAPES THAT ARE UNIVERSAL. I DECONSTRUCT AND COMBINE THEM TO CREATE A LANGUAGE OF LINE, COLOR, AND TEXTURE WHICH I HOPE WILL BE PLEASING TO THE EYE. SOMETIMES MY STORIES HAVE MEANING, EACH SYMBOL REPRESENTATIVE. SOMETIMES THEY ARE MERELY DESIGN ELEMENTS, MEANT TO BE APPRECIATED BY THE EYE ON A PURELY SENSUAL LEVEL. CREATING BEAUTY FOR ITS OWN SAKE, AS PROTECTION AGAINST A HARSH WORLD, IS ONE OF THE MAIN REASONS I AM PLEASED TO BE WORKING AS AN ARTIST IN THIS MEDIUM."

-Ellen Marsh

"WHEN I BEGIN TO THINK ABOUT THE DESIGN OF A GARMENT, I START WITH THE FABRIC. I AM COMPLETELY INSPIRED BY THE SURFACE OF THE CLOTH. IT DETERMINES EVERYTHING ABOUT THE PIECE, FROM THE DRAPE TO THE VISUAL EFFECT. I RECEIVE THE FABRIC FROM ELLEN IN THE MAIL. MOST OF THE TIME WHEN I OPEN A SHIPMENT OF CLOTH, THE CONTENTS ARE A COMPLETE SURPRISE. DESCRIPTIONS OVER THE TELEPHONE ARE NEVER ENOUGH TO PREPARE ME FOR WHAT HAPPENS WHEN I ACTUALLY SEE THE FABRIC FOR THE FIRST TIME. I CAN SMELL CALIFORNIA IN THE CLOTH AND DELVE INTO THE POSSIBILITIES THE FABRIC EVOKES."

-Robin McKay

Left:

Ellen Marsh and Robin McKay, *Moon Warrior*, 1996; silk charmeuse; itajimi (clamped) and arashi shibori; black silk georgette tank dress.

Photo: Wit McKay

Opposite page:

Ellen Marsh and Robin McKay, *Red Bird (Transparencies Collection)*, 2000; silk organza; discharge paste printed; black georgette silk tank dress.

Photo: Wit McKay

The idea that artists on
separate coasts are able to synchronize their energies to make collaborative pieces is itself a novelty. The fact that those people happen to be sisters is even more unusual. Ellen Marsh and Robin McKay agree that their collaboration works because of the tried-and-true trust each has for the other's distinctly different contribution to the process.

When Marsh was attending the California College of Arts and Crafts in Oakland as a graduate student in textiles, she dropped out because the demands of being a student conflicted with the work that she and her sister were already creating and selling. A self-taught surface designer, Marsh's cloth initiates the creative process from which McKay's designs evolve. After the cloth is sent to McKay, the two explore ideas back and forth over the phone and via email, with the understanding that the final word on construction is McKay's realm, while the design of the cloth is Marsh's territory. Says McKay, "We often feel that our work is incomplete without the addition of the other....We are critical or our [own] work and accepting of each other's work."

The balance that they strike is reflected in the understated beauty of their pieces. Marsh's layered, collagelike designs on silk are achieved through a number of processes (used alone or in combination) that she views as her "painter's palette." She names a few: arashi shibori (Japanese pole dyeing), itajimi (Japanese shape resist), rozome (Japanese wax resist), screening with discharge paste, and thickened dye printing. She works from a vocabulary of simplified natural forms and geometric images that are played off one another to create visual interest and resolution.

When McKay responds to Marsh's designs, sometimes the fabric is made to fit a specific pattern, but more often, she works out a design after juxtaposing various pieces. "I arrange and rearrange the pieces until the composition is in place in my visual mind," she continues. After this period of composing, the improvisational process continues in the sewing, as she cuts and com-

bines certain pieces to make a whole. Because of their spontaneous methods of working, it is impossible for Marsh and McKay to replicate a piece.

McKay talks about the labor-intensive operation of making one piece at a time and notes that she and her sister are looking at possibilities for translating some of the fabric designs into a more production-oriented product that could be used for interiors. "We intend to expand our business and at the same time remain true to the spirit of the process by remaining studio-based," she says. Their bicoastal operation, Studio E, is dedicated to the memory of their grandmother Elsie, who was a weaver and an artist.

Opposite page:
Robin McKay and Ellen Marsh, *Magic Geometry in Amber (Transparencies Collection)*, 1999; silk organza; discharge paste printed and itajimi (clamped); silk chiffon tank dress, arashi shibori.
Photo: Wit McKay

Above, left:
Robin McKay and Ellen Marsh, *Black Sunflower (Transparencies Collection)*, 1999; silk organza; discharge paste printed with brush-stroked wax; black silk georgette tank dress.
Photo: Wit McKay

Below, left:
Robin McKay and Ellen Marsh, *Magic Geometry in Natural (Transparencies Collection)*, 1998; silk organza; discharge paste printed and itajimi; black silk georgette tank dress.
Photo: Wit McKay

MIKE & STEVE
KANE & SELLS

NEWLAND, NORTH CAROLINA

"ONE IS ALWAYS THINKING ABOUT ART IF ONE IS AN ARTIST. IT'S JUST THE WAY IT IS. IT IS TOUGH TO BE AN ARTIST AND A BUSINESSPERSON, BECAUSE YOU HAVE TO BE GROUNDED TO BE A BUSINESSPERSON, AND ARTISTS ARE USUALLY UP IN THE CLOUDS! YOU HAVE TO LEARN HOW TO BE EXCITED AND IN THE CLOUDS AND THEN GROUND YOURSELF ...."

Left:

Mike Kane and Steve Sells, *Woodgrain Blocks Kimono*, 2001; silk chiffon; arashi shibori discharge, itajimi discharge dyed.

Photo: John F. Cooper. Model: Julie Zeger

Above:

Mike Kane and Steve Sells, *Silver Woodgrain Bias-Cut Dress and Swing Coat*, 1999; silk, rayon satin; arashi shibori devoré, ombré dyed.

Photo: John F. Cooper. Model: Julie Zeger

Opposite page:

Mike Kane and Steve Sells, *Silver Shards Kimono*, 2001; silk, rayon satin; arashi shibori devoré, mechanical resist devoré, dyed.

Photo: John F. Cooper. Model: Julie Zeger

The collaborative work of
Mike Kane and Steve Sells is a reflection of a balance they seek in life. Their partnership lends a push-pull aspect to their creative process, resulting in work that has been praised by critics and purchased by many.

The interesting tension that is manifested in their arashi shibori surfaces conveys open-ended discovery while bearing clear evidence of years spent learning and practicing the technical aspects of their medium. The reference of nature is apparent when looking at their work, which bears rhythmic but varied patterning resembling the intricate design of lichens on rocks or the hypnotic movement of the ocean.

Both artists began their careers as painters. They first learned about resist dyeing by doing intricate tie-dye on shirts that they sold at a local farmer's market. They quickly discovered the dichotomy that often exists between doing satisfying creative work and making money from it. The amount of work that they put into each piece far exceeded what they could earn.

They decided to put their energies into a different context by experimenting with other fabrics—a process that eventually led them to the decision to create more sophisticated clothing. Their understanding of the art-to-wear field was aided by smart preparation. They haunted the best shows and fielded questions to successful artists, seeking out those who seemed to be the happiest with what they were doing. They discovered that the artists who were repetitively "cranking out" work to fill orders were often disenchanted. They vowed not to take this road and instead find a way to retain an edge of excitement in their business and their art.

So far, they have managed to keep the process and the work fresh, in part by resisting production work and doing one-of-a-kind pieces. Their sincerity and enthusiasm attract the attention of both customers and colleagues. When asked why many of their colleagues look to them for advice and inspiration, they explain their noncompetitive philosophy of sharing:

> We have tried to influence lots of people. We love doing that. It's kind of a game with us. We think that the more creative everyone is, the better off we all are as a society. And we are not concerned about competition....We are usually so excited about what we're doing that when we are telling people, they get excited and go do something new and fresh.

Their interest has been ongoing since they began creating clothing more than a decade ago. At an early point in their career, they discovered the technique of arashi shibori through Yoshika Wada's highly influential book called *Shibori: The Inventive Art of Japanese Shaped Resist Dyeing* (Harper and Row, 1983). After experimenting with many techniques in the book, they developed their own variation of the resist-dyeing technique that has become their signature. Simply put, the fabric is intricately wrapped and compressed around a long piece of plastic pipe before being bound with kite string. They first used this technique to dye scarves, then created kimono-inspired garments. Later they added coats, jackets, dresses, blouses, and other clothing to their repertoire.

Over the past few years, they have combined the discharge process of devoré with shibori. Beginning with silk rayon velvet, they use a brush to apply an acid etching chemical that is later removed on high heat in a gas dryer. This process takes away the rayon pile of the velvet, leaving behind the diaphanous silk. Combined with arashi shibori's unusual patterning, it adds another dimension to the surface by contrasting texture and depth as well as opacity.

The patterns of shibori in their work seem as if they have required the passage of long periods of time. Simultaneously, the images give the impression that they are still evolving—ever so slowly and patiently—into something deeper and more beautiful.

Opposite page:

Mike Kane and Steve Sells, *Woodgrain Wrap-Dress and Field Jacket*, 2000; silk chiffon; arashi shibori discharge dyed.

Photo: John F. Cooper. Model: Julie Zeger

Left:

Mike Kane and Steve Sells, *Earth-Tone Koi Coat*, 1998; silk crepe de chine; arashi shibori dyed, discharged, over dyed, ombré dyed; pieced.

Photo: John F. Cooper. Model: Julie Zeger

Below:

Mike Kane and Steve Sells, *Basket Weave Coat*, 2001; silk rayon velvet; devoré (hand etched), remaining pile discharge dyed.

Photo: John F. Cooper. Model: Julie Zeger

JOAN MCGEE

SARASOTA, FLORIDA

"BASICALLY, I AM NOT AFRAID TO TRY ANY-
THING. I GET AN IDEA, AND THEN, IN MY
MIND, I ORGANIZE THE BEST WAY TO EXECUTE
IT. SOMETIMES I DREAM ABOUT THINGS, AND
WAKE UP AND TRY THEM. SINCE WHAT I DO IS
A PASSION, I AM ALWAYS THINKING ABOUT
HOW TO MAKE MORE BEAUTIFUL, UNIQUE
CLOTH AND CLOTHING DESIGNS. I HAVE
ALWAYS FELT THAT MY BRAIN WILL RECORD
MY SUCCESS AS WELL AS MY FAILURE, AND IT
DOES THIS FOR ME. IF A 'NEW' IDEA DOESN'T
WORK OUT, I TRY AGAIN."

Opposite page, left:
**Joan McGee, Untitled, 2000; silk/polyester; heat
transfer, fused fabric (jacket); silk/polyester;
pole-wrapped, pleated with shibori techniques (skirt).**
Photo: Christopher Bunn. Model: Evia Marrison

Opposite page, right:
**Joan McGee, *Cleopatra*, 2000; silk/lamé; heat transfer,
pleated (dress); silk/lamé; pole-wrapped, knotted with
shibori techniques, overdyed black (scarf).**
Photo: Christopher Bunn. Model: Evia Marrison

Right:
**Joan McGee, *Sunrise*, 2001; silk/chenille; hand dyed,
handwoven; silk/satin (lining); shibori.**
Photo: Christopher Bunn. Model: Evia Marrison

If you look back at the career of Joan McGee, you'll notice one theme: she is obsessively experimental with cloth. The range of techniques that she has undertaken and successfully incorporated into her work illustrates a fearless desire to constantly evolve. Her body of work shows a consistent love of color and texture while incorporating handwovens, silk shibori, natural dyed silk velvet, and other approaches. Although cloth is her primary love, the designs of her clothing are equally as creative.

She is never completely satisfied with her work and always sees something new that pushes her on— whether it is something from her everyday environment or an outside influence such as seeing new yarns and fabrics in Europe. A consistent sense of drama in her work stems from the experimental nature of her fabrics.

This love of clothing began when she was a child who always wanted to be a designer and make her own cloth. Born and raised in Seattle, she discovered commercial dyes in junior high school and made clothing out of her original fabrics, because she wasn't particularly impressed with what she saw in stores.

This early interest was interrupted by what seemed to be a more practical decision to study sociology and become a social worker. After a year of working, she earned a graduate degree in special education from San Jose State University in California. She taught school for 10 years—always using art to teach life skills to her students.

She returned to her childhood love "in earnest" after her three children left the nest. In 1976, she began dyeing and weaving her own yarns, making rugs and tapestries for many years. A few years later, she began selling handwoven jackets, and found a niche in clothing. To accompany some of her clients' desires for blouses to go with her handwoven suits, she traveled to Italy to find unique fabrics. She discovered shibori on a trip to Japan in 1992, and a later trip to Venice, Italy, and the Fortuni Palace convinced her that she wanted to incorporate shibori into her work. Today, she still makes a yearly trip to Europe to buy fabrics and often enhances them with shibori or other techniques to make them unique.

She is fascinated with the endless variations that shibori offers, and focuses a lot of her attention on this technique. The loom is still a part of her equipment, but her husband now weaves cloth from the yarns that she dyes. As she says: "There are so many things to do with cloth that I will never in my lifetime get around to it all."

Opposite page:
Joan McGee, *Deep Forest*, 1993; silk; board-clamped, discharged, pole-wrapped, overdyed with shibori techniques.
Photo: Jane Weitel. Model: Marcy Mellish

Above:
Joan McGee, Untitled, 2000; silk/satin; board-clamped, discharged, pole-wrapped, overdyed, knotted (shibori).
Photo: Christopher Bunn. Model: Evia Marrison

Above right:
Joan McGee, Untitled, 2000; polyester with woven metal thread; heat transferred.
Photo: Christopher Bunn. Model: Evia Marrison

Right:
Joan McGee, *Tiger*, 1994; silk; pole-wrapped, discharged with shibori techniques.
Photo: Christopher Bunn. Model: Evia Marrison

KARREN K. BRITO

YELLOW SPRINGS, OHIO

"I LOVE TEXTILES WITH PATTERNS AND TEXTURES. THE PATTERNS THAT I lIKE AND CAN LOOK AT TIME AND TIME AGAIN AND STILL SEE NEW ELEMENTS HAVE BOTH A REPEATING ELEMENT AND AN UNPREDICTABLE ELEMENT. THE REPEATING ELEMENT GIVES RHYTHM AND PREDICTABILITY, LULLING ME INTO THINKING I UNDERSTAND THE PATTERN. THEN ONE OF THE UNPREDICTABLE ELEMENTS APPEARS AND CHANGES MY THINKING. THE BALANCE BETWEEN THE PREDICTABLE AND THE UNPREDICTABLE ELEMENTS CREATES A WONDERFUL PATTERN, SO THAT ONE SEES NEW VISUAL RELATIONSHIPS AGAIN AND AGAIN."

Right:
Karren K. Brito, *Dawn Mist*, 2000; silk; capped and arashi shibori, glass beads.
Photo: Joe Van De Hatert

Opposite page:
Karren K. Brito, *Autumn Leaves*, 2000; large feather-pleated boa; silk; arashi shibori, glass beads.
Photo: Joe Van De Hatert

More than a decade ago,
Karren K. Brito left the security of her day job—a prestigious position as a research chemist and professor at Antioch University—to pursue the out-of-the-mainstream life of a handweaver. What led a woman with a Ph.D. in chemistry to find her true calling in a seemingly unrelated field?

Brito learned to sew, embroider, and crochet at an early age. Her natural fascination with textile arts became submerged, but never died. Her bio gives a quick nod at explaining her first career choice: "Sputnik convinced the American people and Karren that the United States needed more scientists."

Nevertheless, she found herself using money earned working one summer at NASA to buy a loom. While still teaching, she pursued her weaving on the side. In 1983, she began to market her handwoven garments before taking a partial leap of faith several years later when she cut back on her class load. Several years later, she left her position in the academic community to work full time as a fiber artist.

Her background in chemistry gave her a natural understanding of and willingness to experiment with dyes. Eventually, she found her interest in dyeing fitted to the silk shibori work for which she is well-known today.

She studied traditional shibori at Penland School of Crafts in North Carolina. In arashi shibori, undyed cloth is tied around a pole (traditionally wood, now plastic) before immersing it in dye. In a variation of this idea, she often dyes her silk first, then pleats and folds it before discharging the fabric to remove some of the color. This subtractive process is often followed by the addition of color through overdyeing. She feels that her processes strike a balance between the predictable and the accidental, resulting in a multi-faceted surface coloration.

The lightweight silk that she uses is perfectly suited for the dyeing and folding processes she employs. Through intricate double feather-pleats, she transforms almost weightless fabric into shawls and scarves that appear

sculptural when supported by the body. Her largest shibori pieces are floor-length opera shawls that contain many yards of silk, all pleated and wrapped at one time. Shawls are her most popular item because they can be worn as scarves or opened out to wrap around the body. Once on the wearer, movement causes them to change and shimmer, partially because many of her pieces are dyed so that there is a color contrast between the top and bottom pleats. Many of her pieces are finished with glass beads that provide weight and decorative emphasis to the garments.

In a 1998 article written by Kathleen McCann for *FIBERARTS* (January/February issue), Brito describes her outlook about her work, the market, and her decision to go it on her own in an uncertain profession:

> My life is so much better now. Most inhibitions are inside of us. It takes awhile. You have to be willing to listen to the marketplace and adjust. But either you run your own business or somebody else runs your business. If you want an independent life, you have to take hold of the reins and make it.

Opposite page:
Karren K. Brito, *Red Roses Tango*, 2000; opera shawl and large feather-pleated boa; silk; capped and arashi shibori, glass beads.
Photo: Joe Van De Hatert

Right:
Karren K. Brito, *Toast Shawl*, 1996; silk; arashi shibori, glass beads.
Photo: Eric Owens

GENEVIÈVE
DION
DENVER, COLORADO

"SHIBORI IS A VERY EXCITING PROCESS BECAUSE IT MAY BE USED AS AN INTEGRAL PART OF THE FINAL DESIGN. RATHER THAN DESIGNING OR EMBELLISHING A PIECE OF CLOTH, AND THEN USING IT TO CREATE A GARMENT OR ACCESSORY, SHIBORI CAN BE USED TO SHAPE THE PIECE FROM THE START TO THE FINISH. WHAT DISTINGUISHES AND MOVES MY WORK BEYOND TRADITIONAL BOUNDARIES IS THAT I SCULPT THE ENTIRE PIECE USING SHIBORI SO THAT THE TRANSITION BETWEEN FORM AND TEXTURE ARE INTEGRATED...MY PROCESS ALLOWS PERMANENT AND IRREVERSIBLE SHAPING OF PURE SILK."

Opposite page and right:
Geneviève Dion, *Velvet Opera Cape with Hand-beaded Tassels*, 1993; shibori-dyed using *ori nui* technique.
Photo: Kim Cook

Geneviève Dion's first mentor
was her grandmother, Marie-Louise Picard, who encouraged her to design and sew. By the age of 11, she was making and selling shoes and handbags in her native Quebec City, Canada. Later, she studied art and design, and planned to become a shoe designer after studying with Gaza Bowen at San Francisco State Unversity.

In 1989, her direction changed when she took a workshop with world-renowned shibori artist and academic Yoshika Wada. She was enamored with the process of shibori and found it fitted her aesthetic inclinations. Wada encouraged her to experiment with the resist-dye technique in order to come up with her own interpretations. As a result, her work in shibori was chosen to represent the United States in the 1991 Textile Design contest in Tokyo, Japan. Encouraged by this acknowledgment of her work, she turned all of her attention to creating works that incorporated innovative shibori processes. By 1999, she was exhibiting in Santiago, Chile, at the well-known International Shibori Symposium.

Dion notes that the "memory" left by the folding, clamping, or stitching prior to dyeing is the starting point for all of her designs. "I use the three-dimensionality of shibori to inspire and shape the pieces," she notes. She often begins with unprocessed Japanese silk that is stiff and feels like tissue paper. Before scouring the silk, which shrinks it by 50 percent in width, she sculpts the fabric into textures (to be used at the neck of the garment, on the sleeves, etc). After it is scoured and shrunk, it is dyed with a shibori process. The texture is permanent, and the final garments can be washed and the texture will remain.

Shibori provides her with endless possibilities. Besides working with silks, she uses a knitting technique to create a double-sided fabric in which complementary threads have a presence on each side. Open areas in the fabric that occur naturally in construction are interspersed with strips of velvet. Then the fabric is dyed using a shibori process.

Looking back, she recalls that she was always interested in making functional pieces. "I like things that work...I always tended to make things that could be used." she says. Dion's textural creations make a compelling argument for the vast possibilities of integrating the experimental nature of cutting-edge art with the functional aspects of clothing.

Opposite page:
Geneviève Dion, *Hand-knotted Velvet Coat,***1995;**
stitched-resisted and shibori dyed.
Photo: Donna Miller

Above:
Geneviève Dion, *Silk Deco Dress* **(detail), 2000; one-piece**
design, scoured and *ori nui* **shibori-dyed, sculpted gores.**
Photo: Kim Cook

Right:
Geneviève Dion, *Silk Deco Dress,* **2000; one-piece design,**
scoured and *ori nui* **shibori-dyed, sculpted gores.**
Photo: Kim Cook

MARK THOMAS

SAN FRANCISCO, CALIFORNIA

"I HAVE ALWAYS HAD AN OBSESSIVE DRIVE TO BE CREATIVE....LEARNING TO WORK WITH COLOR AND ITS INTERACTION IS A NEVER-ENDING CHALLENGE AND CURIOSITY. THERE ARE MANY THINGS THAT ENCOURAGE ME TO KEEP PUSHING THE BOUNDARIES OF MY WORK—A GREAT LOVE FOR ART AND NATURE, A LOVE OF TOOLMAKING AND DEVISING NEW TECHNIQUES, A FASCINATION WITH DYE CHEMISTRY, LEARNING NEW WAYS TO FIT A THREE-DIMENSIONAL FIGURE THROUGH THE PATTERN-MAKING PROCESS...AND, ON THE PERSONAL SIDE, A STRONG DESIRE TO BE RECOGNIZED AND RESPECTED AMONGST MY PEERS...AND A STRONG FEAR OF AN ORDINARY EXISTENCE."

Left:
Mark Thomas, *Coat*, 2000; velvet; shibori, hand-painted gradations.
Photo: Bryan Northup. Model: Traci Caybut

Mark Thomas' resistance to an "ordinary existence" began when he was young. At a tender age, he felt totally uprooted when his parents moved him and his seven brothers and sisters from St. Louis, Missouri, to "a small nowhere town" in the Arizona desert. The stark desert landscape shocked him into a realization of his need to be surrounded by color.

His parents bought him paint sets, and he learned to make his own varied palette. Next, he discovered fabric dye, and unplanned occurrences on his mother's shag carpeting taught him "what happens when you lay a little red over avocado green and royal blue."

In a natural progression of things, he ordered tie-dye booklets advertised on the back of grocery store dye boxes and became a "tie-dye addict." He planned to become an artist but settled on the idea of pursuing fashion illustration and design. He moved to California and saved money to attend school. After a year at the Fashion Institute of Design and Merchandising in Los Angeles, California, he was dissatisfied with the lack of emphasis on the technical aspects of design and switched to the Los Angeles Trade-Technical College, where he honed his skills at pattern making, grading, and illustrating.

Before finishing the degree, he accepted a job as a design assistant with Oscar-winning Hollywood costume designer Jean-Pierre Dorleac. He worked on a panoply of projects but was most affected when he observed the construction of costumes for the movie *Blade Runner*. They were "past fashion but still wearable," he

Right:
Mark Thomas, *Coat*, 1999; velvet; blockprinting, discharge/overdye stripe, hand-painted gradations.
Photo: Bryan Northup. Model: Traci Caybut

remembers. He began to think about the possibility of "apparel as an art form." A couple of years later, he sat beside a woman in an airport who was knitting an unusual sweater. When he asked her about her creation, she told him about an art-to-wear gallery in San Francisco called Obiko. Soon after that, he went to Obiko and met the owner, Sandra Sakata, who fed his enthusiasm for a newly discovered possibility for his creativity.

Above:
**Mark Thomas, *Jacket*, 1999; velvet;
blockprinting, discharge/overdye strip,
hand-painted gradations.**
Photo Bryan Northup. Model Traci Caybut

Right:
**Mark Thomas, *Jacket*,
1999; velvet; discharge/overdye
stripe, blockprinting.**
Photo: Bryan Northup. Model: Traci Caybut

He moved to San Francisco to pursue a career in art-to-wear, and by 1984 was experimenting with hand-dyeing and painting silk. He sold work to Obiko, Bergdorf Goodman, and private clientele. By the late 1980s, he tired of a seemingly commercial scene and considered returning to school to study fine art. But when another opportunity presented itself to work for fashion designer Catherine Bacon, he took it. Through collaborating with Bacon to produce hand-dyed textiles for her works, he was able to disconnect himself from marketing concerns and explore a variety of design techniques and applications. After nine years, he exhausted this experience and made a resolution that he would "take [his own] little piggies to market."

In 1999, he entered the art-to-wear marketplace with his hand-painted velvet coats and separates. He has devised an effective nonimmersion shibori technique using paintbrushes, squeeze bottles, and spray bottles. His work has been well-received, and he has found a supportive community. He constantly works on the challenge of maintaining his "artistic integrity" without "cutting corners and producing formulaic responses because it's more profitable."

Modernist painters have been his biggest influence, and he wanders the galleries, museums, and botanical gardens of San Francisco to feed his obsession with color and design. The compelling abstractions on velvet that he now creates lend meaning to his years of searching and questioning.

Right:
Mark Thomas, *Coat*, 2000; velvet; shibori, hand-painted gradations.
Photo: Bryan Northup. Model: Traci Caybut

MICHELLE MURRAY

ST. AUGUSTINE, FLORIDA

"THIS WORK IN SHIBORI GIVES ME THE LATITUDE FOR PASSIONATE COLOR PLAY. I FAVOR SATURATED COLORS BECAUSE THEY ACCOMMODATE THE REDUCTION TECHNIQUES THAT I AM CURRENTLY USING, AS WELL AS SATISFY EXCESSIVE TENDENCIES IN MY PERSONALITY. REPLICATION [OF ANY PIECE] IS DIFFICULT BECAUSE I REJECT ANY SORT OF FORMULAE IN THE DYE PROCESS. I BEGIN BY CONTEMPLATING FAVORITE 'MOOD-STORY' IMAGES (E.G., 'CEREMONIAL ROBES' OR 'BOHEMIAN CAMP'). TO EACH STORY IMAGE ARE ADDED VERY SUBJECTIVE COLOR NOTIONS (E.G., 'MONASTIC' OR 'FOREST'). THEN, BEGINNING WITH ONLY A LIMITED PALETTE OF HUES, I ENGAGE THESE IMAGES IN THE CONCOCTIONS [DYES] I MIX. ALTHOUGH THE PROCESS IS CONTEMPLATIVE, AN OBSERVER MIGHT DESCRIBE THE ACTIVITY AS FRENZIED! PAINTING IS THE EXCITING PART, BUT THE SILK MUST BE TAKEN THROUGH A NUMBER OF OTHER PROCESSES: STEAMING, WASHING, IRONING, AND PLEATING. OFTEN THE CYCLE IS REPEATED MORE THAN ONCE ON A SINGLE PIECE."

Above:
**Michelle Murray, *Organza Scales Wrap*, 2001;
silk organza; dyed and hand pleated,
arashi shibori, overdyed.**

Photo: Root Photography

Left:
**Michelle Murray, *Cinnamon Moss Scales Wrap*, 2000;
silk habotai; handpainted, hand pleated,
arashi shibori, overdyed.**

Photo: Root Photography

Opposite page:
**Michelle Murray, *Smoked Organza Tabard with Scale
Pleated Hip Belt*, 2000; silk organza; arashi shibori
with hand-manipulated variations,
hand pleated, dyed.**

Photo: Root Photography

Michelle Murray's inventive
work satisfies her early inclinations toward both painting
and sculpture. When she was a child growing up in
Southern California, her mother provided her with a gen-
erous box of crayons which she "smeared around" like
most children. But she also thoughtfully gave "names
and detailed personality traits to each hue while enact-
ing dramas around them." She despised dolls, until she
discovered clever little troll dolls that she dressed with a
wardrobe of self-devised costumes. As a young woman,
ready-to-wear was not interesting enough for her, and
she created her own outfits for special parties.

Admittedly rebellious, she dropped out of college at the
University of Washington in 1971 because of a prefer-
ence for "anti-war demonstrations and other adventures." (She returned to the university 20 years later to
complete her B.S. in psychology and a B.F.A. in painting.) Some of those adventures included hitchhiking
across the United States and Mexico, traveling to Asia,
Africa, and South America, and cruising the South Pacific
for two years on a sailboat.

By the time she was in her late twenties, she "craved"
to do something with her life, and an old friend in
Seattle suggested that they learn to weave rugs. She
successfully earned a living doing this for about a
decade, then went on to produce handwoven wearable
art in the 1980s, which by 1987 was shown on the
runway of the New York Wholesale Fashion Mart.

The turning point in her artistic career came when she
studied at Haystack Mountain School of Crafts in Maine
with Ana Lisa Hedstrom, who introduced her to the
basics of shibori sans the "formulaic spoonfeeding" of
many teachers. She credits Hedstrom with pushing her
and other students to evolve in their own directions with
the medium. Shibori fit her need for more direct expression, and she eventually gave up weaving.

Although she doesn't credit herself with inventing a particular way of doing shibori, she has developed her own idiosyncratic way of approaching it. She mixes her own dyes from primary hues and then rolls out her canvas of white silk on a table before improvisationally painting on "large color fields." After the silk is dried and the dyes are set, the silk is washed again to remove the excess. These "wildly colored silks" are then folded and pressed into large pleats and shapes—sometimes stitched—before being laid against a large plastic sewer pipe.

Thread is wound around and around the pipe, and she manipulates the fabric at chosen places with variations of tucking and pinching. Periodically the fabric is pushed to one end of the pipe, and she may choose to twist it to change the pleat details. (She admits that the "exceedling meticulous pleating" makes her crazy!) The entire piece is compressed and bound by threads, and the pipe with contents intact, is dipped into a large discharge bath that strips out some of the color.

After this process, she paints color back onto the stripped portions of the pleats. Eventually, the fabric is washed and dried to set the pleats. If she isn't content with the results, she sometimes irons out the pleats and dyes over the fabric with another layer of patterning, or she might choose to add pleats in another direction to create extremely high texture of up to four inches.

She finds it a challenge to strike a balance between exploring new ideas and undertaking the time-consuming method of her work. When she finally gets this precious time, she "tears her studio to shreds...experimenting with so many long-held and frustrated ideas." This process entails "many disastrous results at first," she says, "then something clicks—usually straight from concept to existence."

CARTER SMITH

NAHANT, MASSACHUSETTS

"I DO [SHIBORI] BECAUSE I LOVE TO DO IT, NOT BECAUSE IT IS A BUSINESS. I DO IT IN SPITE OF THE BUSINESS. THE INSPIRATION COMES FROM MY DREAMS. I AM CONTINUALLY WRITING THINGS DOWN AS THEY COME TO ME AND THEN RUNNING THE IDEAS THROUGH THE STUDIO. THERE IS NO END TO WHAT YOU CAN DO OR CREATE IN THIS FIELD. THE POSSIBILITIES ARE ENDLESS. THE OPENESS OF THE PROCESS IS WHAT KEEPS ME GOING."

Opposite page:
Carter Smith, *Secrets* (K dresses); 2000; silk and rayon, black cut satin; shibori pattern.
Photo: Joan Emm

Right:
Carter Smith, *Dance Shadows* (scarf coat and kimono); 1999; double georgette, silk; shibori.
Photo: Joan Emm

If Carter Smith had not found shibori as an outlet for his intense, obsessive need to explore, he might have been a number of other things that one can only speculate about. If he'd been born in the time before the discovery of America, he might have been on the ship that first bumped into the rocky coast of New England. If he had been born in the days before flight, he might have become an Orville or Wilbur Wright.

He's the type of person who, first and foremost, impresses you with his ability to make things happen. He is an entrepreneurial artist. In addition to an innate artistic ability, Smith has been successful because he is able to constantly reinvent his work. As testimony to his skill at keeping things moving, he has had a successful career doing what he loves for more than 35 years.

His work as a "master" of shibori has provided him with a vehicle to express his ever-evolving sense of himself and his place in the world. Shibori, with its infinite number of possibilities, is a meaningful way to address his desire to be viewed as both highly individual and unique.

Smith began his road to silken glory in 1965 at age 19 when he learned to tie-dye from his mother. He took to the medium as if it had always been his and created a business selling his work that supported him while he earned his M.F.A. in sculpture from the University of California at Santa Cruz. He continued to build his business around creating tie-dye fabric that was made into scarves, wall hangings, or sold to designers to make into fashion.

As he looks back on this period in his career, he notes that he believes he was "doing it then for all the wrong reasons." Because he was focused on the money and the production aspects of his work, he eventually lost the excitement of learning. His solution: He dropped out and worked as a carpenter for a couple of years.

By 1985, he was working at his art again, this time with a determination to keep it fresh. He remembers:

"I started playing with it the way I had done in the beginning, and used the energy of the surprise of opening each piece to rekindle the flame. I did it again for the passion, the excitement, the art." While "playing" at his work, he discovered something important: "Focus on the creative energy and the joy of creating, and it will work itself out in the economy. When you focus [too much] on making a living, it becomes more of a job." From that time forward, he embraced the unresolved nature of experimentation and undertook to "perfect" the art of shibori, which served as a natural segue out of tie-dye and into his reinvention of himself.

By the late 1980s, he realized that he would never obtain the recognition that he felt he deserved by making fabrics for designers who "did not want to let anyone know who created the fabric." Undaunted by his lack of knowledge about pattern-making and sewing, he designed his own simple patterns and hired several seamstresses to assemble his creations. He soon discovered that it was much easier to sell clothing than wall hangings.

Smith experimented with many dyeing techniques, but found that he liked the effects of discharging the folded, pleated, and bound fabric. In areas where the color is removed, he added back bright fiber-reactive dyes through overdyeing—a technique that led to his signature look. As he tries to simplify his present-day process for the uninitiated, he generalizes by saying that his work "involves a lot of layering and combinations of techniques" over the same piece of fabric.

Stepping out into the art-to-wear arena as a designer pushed him into a much higher category of recognition. Now in his 50s, he speaks about his work from a place of introspection and experience. A ready purveyor of his life's philosophy, he often describes creativity as related to the willingness to let go—to lose control of the process. In line with this recurring theme, he says with Spinoza-like reflection: "It's not what you know, but what you don't know." He gives much of the credit to his medium, thinking of himself as the tool for channeling the most

mysterious aspects of the creative process—the ones that don't lend themselves to articulation. In assertion of his place in the process, he intones: "The spirit is what happens in the piece, not what you do."

Smith, unlike some artists who find it difficult to talk about their work and their accomplishments, unapologetically enumerates the statistics of his expansive undertakings since he began his concentration on shibori: "My guess is that over the past 15 years I have explored close to 3,000 shibori-related techniques, and over the 36 years of my full career I have dyed close to 200,000 yards of fabric, mostly silk." He notes that he uses "about 40 techniques which can be used in millions of combinations...."

Only millions? In the spirit of Carter Smith, the more appropriate word might be "billions."

Carter Smith, _K Dress;_ 1995; double georgette silk; shibori. Necklace by Susan Green.
Photo: Susan Schilling

Carter Smith, _On Fire_ (K dress); 2000; satin, silk, and rayon; shibori. Jewelry by Susan Green.
Photo: Joan Emm

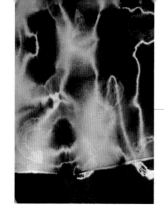

KAY DISBROW

WOODSTOCK, NEW YORK

"I FEEL AS THOUGH I'M DOING WHAT I'M SUPPOSED TO BE DOING WITH MY LIFE WHEN I CREATE VISUALLY, ESPECIALLY ON CLOTH. IT IS VERY SATISFYING WHEN SOMEBODY FEELS BETTER ABOUT THEM-SELVES WEARING SOMETHING THAT I HAVE MADE. I HAVE HAD PEOPLE EXPERI-ENCE HEALING THOUGHTS THAT I HAVE INVESTED IN A GARMENT. FOR ME, IT IS A SPIRITUAL DISCIPLINE TO MEDITATE ON BENEFICIAL PRINCIPLES WHILE I WORK."

For Kay Disbrow, one of the most satisfying things about her work is the connection that she feels with those who end up wearing it. She draws her inspiration from nature and has spent her career learning and growing, always seeking to express her fascination with the textures, patterns, and colors of life.

The road of discovery has led her from being a sculptor working in plastic and metal to a fiber artist working in painting and dyeing techniques. In the innovative atmos-phere of San Franciso and the Bay Area during the 1960s, she studied sculpture at the University of California at Berkeley and at San Francisco State before discovering that she could translate her artistic inclina-tions into fiber.

Encouragement from a weaving teacher, who was adamant that she not think simplistically about weaving as "yardage," opened her mind to the creation of sculp-tural forms on the loom. She did this for several years before her interest in fiber took precedence.

During the 1970s, her activities centered on fiber—dressmaking, doing patchwork, and running a vintage clothing business that specialized in silk velvets. Eventually, she began making clothing. For many years, into the 1980s, she made quilted jackets, including ones made from antique fabrics, that became her signa-ture. She received so much positive response to her work that she decided to go into business for herself making what she prefers to call "art clothing."

During the 1990s, shibori and dyeing fabric drew her attention. She studied books about shibori, but the key to her learning came through a class with Joan Morris. Overwhelmed in the beginning with the complexity of the chemistry with its seemingly endless dyes and effects, she found her own method for learning. She patiently experimented and experimented, asked ques-tions of colleagues, and watched instructional videos that were available in order to teach herself.

Opposite page:
Kay Disbrow, *Raku*, 1998; silk and rayon velvet; dextrin resist, dye painted.
Photo: Peter Kricker
Model: Emily Barzin

Right:
Kay Disbrow, *Black & White*, 1997; jacquard silk crepes; arashi shibori, mokumé shibori, capping, pieced (kimono coat).
Photo: Peter Kricker
Model: Emily Barzin

Today, she uses a combination of techniques to create her work that include several types of shibori, painting on fabric, burnout (devoré), and a dextrin resist. Some of her most interesting pieces have resulted from her experimentation with dextrin resist—a vegetable paste made of potato (dextrin) powder. To undertake this technique, fabric is stretched and anchored to a table and the cooled paste is spread on selected areas. When the resist dries, it crackles. Thickened dyes are spread over the paste, allowing the color to penetrate the cracks. The dextrin is eventually removed to reveal the spontaneous patterns created by the natural course revealed in the drying.

Her love of this technique led her to create a series of pieces that she compares to the ceramic technique of raku. Her work has been influenced by many things, including thousands of glazed pieces of pottery that she has studied over the years. From her painted and dyed fabrics she often makes a garment that she has dubbed as the "kimono coat"—a westernized, suited-for-many version of the kimono with deeper and more fitted armholes, cuffs, and side-seam pockets.

Although she has used vintage fabrics and silks, velvet has been her fabric of choice for many years. Opening an old trunk of her grandmother's and mother's dresses at age 12 first exposed her to the seemingly mysterious properties of velvet—a fascination that remains with her today. She loves its "light-reflective qualities and luminosity." Silk rayon velvet works well for her burnout process as well as for the absorption of her vibrantly colored dyes.

Left:
Kay Disbrow, *Alchemy*, 1998; silk and rayon velvet; arashi shibori, devoré, dye painted, overdyed.
Photo: Peter Kricker. Model: Emily Barzin

Opposite page:
Kay Disbrow, *Autumn Walk*, 2000; silk and rayon velvet; dye painted, images of ferns discharged through photo silk screen.
Photo: Peter Kricker. Model: Emily Barzin

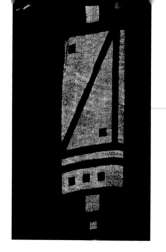

MAUDE ANDRADE

"I AM IMMENSELY FASCINATED WITH HOW THE WORLD DEFINES AND VIEWS ART CATEGORIES....WHY IS A PAINTING ON A GARMENT TREATED SO DIFFERENTLY THAN A PAINTING IN A FRAME HUNG ON THE WALL?....I'M NOT SURE I CONSIDER MYSELF AN ARTIST, AND I KNOW PEOPLE WHO WOULD DEFINITELY NOT CONSIDER ME TO BE AN ARTIST OR MY CLOTHING ART."

Left:

Maude Andrade, *#8/19 Animals*, 1997-98; handwoven rayon chenille; discharge printed.

Photo: John Cooper. Stylist: Peter Brown

Opposite page:

Maude Andrade, *Road to Abiquiu*, 2001; handwoven rayon chenille; discharge shibori, hand dyed; pieced; silk lining.

Photo: John Cooper. Stylist: Peter Brown

If you look up "artist" in one edition of Webster's, you'll find that it defines the word in part as "one who professes and practices an imaginative art." Maude Andrade might not always call herself an artist, but she certainly behaves like one. Her impulses to work out ideas and abstractions on cloth are artistic, definitions notwithstanding.

She grew up in a creative household where she played in the studio of her mother, Jo Diggs, a well-known textile artist. She was influenced by the open, artistic environment of Corrales, New Mexico, in the 1970s. Like her mother, who melds abstract and representational references in her work, Andrade has developed her own symbolic surface language to express her personal intentions.

Academic training in botany and chemistry provided her with the confidence and knowledge to experiment with dye technology. Her treatment of surface references many techniques: discharge printing and painting, elements of photo silk-screening, dyeing, shibori, and freehand painting with dyes. Pattern and color are used to create abstract compositions that come to life on the body of the wearer. Recently, she has begun to paint with oils and make monoprints into which she integrates the textures of fabrics and stitching.

She cites many influences including Asian, Grecian, Egyptian, Minoan, and tribal motifs. A wide traveler of the world, she is guided by her impressions from these experiences, working out her narratives in a world without windows: a studio space in a small industrial park. The dichotomies that fuel her work—order and chaos, chance and control, ancient and modern, dark and light—are a part of her daily life.

Her worldview brims with joy over creating something new, and the energy of relating that to others:

Creating is how I communicate and connect with the world. I create because I have to, because my brain is always working on new ideas, and I get real satisfaction, happiness, or a high, when I create something that people connect with and want in their life. My most successful designs usually come from a place within me that conveys the feelings I remember from a perfect day at the beach with loved ones, or a perfect meal shared with my husband on some small island in Greece—those special times in my life when everything is calm and beautiful.

ELLEN GIENGER

BEND, OREGON

"MY FABRICS ARE HANDPAINTED AND THEN BLOCKPRINTED....I PREFER TO PAINT FREELY, AND BLOCKPRINTING IS IMMEDIATELY GRATIFYING. I LOVE WATCHING IT ALL HAPPEN IN THE MOMENT. I AM NOT A PATIENT PERSON. I LIKE TO KNOW WHAT I AM GETTING WHILE I AM DOING IT...PAINTING FABRIC IS VERY PHYSICAL AND TAKES A LOT OF STRENGTH. I LOVE TO MOVE....AND [MY PROCESS OF PAINTING IS] LIKE A DANCE MOVING AROUND TWO GIGANTIC TABLES."

Right:
Ellen Gienger, *Kesa*, 2000; silk rayon velvets and velvet burnouts; hand painted, printed, pieced, serged, pressed.
Photo: Polara Studios

Opposite page:
Ellen Gienger, *Lion Kesa*, 2001; silk rayon, burnout velvet; hand painted, block printed with fiber-reactive dyes, pieced, serged.
Photo: Ross Chandler

Ellen Gienger seems to move on impulse—both in her art and in her life. In 1989, when she was living in a small town in southern Oregon, she read an article about the work of textile artist Douglas Ram Samuj and was intrigued by the painterly nature of his surface design. Gienger was already making and selling pieced and quilted wearable art at this point, but she sensed a possibility for a collaborative association after seeing his work. She followed her instincts and called the well-known designer in Beverly Hills. The call led her to a life-changing association, and, for the next few years, she created striking clothing from his fabrics.

After Ram Samuj's death in 1994—a painful loss for Gienger—she knew that she could not replace his contribution to her work by finding another textile designer. She rekindled her interest in painting (having studied fine art at the California State University and the School of the Art Institute of Chicago), learned about dyes, and applied her innate talent to creating her own fabrics. During this same period, she relocated to Bend, Oregon, and settled into a warehouse studio on the river.

Her exposure to the late Ram Samuj still influences her aesthetic and her approach to surface design. She uses layers of blockprinting and painting to create dramatic and varied abstract patterning on her fabrics that are played off of one another to contrast forces such as

light and dark, movement and stasis, sheer and opaque.

Today, her work is focused on the use of silks and velvets because of the market for these fabrics, although she has a special love for linens. She works by rolling out a large bolt of fabric on her studio table, and applies color with her blocks and dyes in an improvisational manner that she compares to that of the late painter Jackson Pollock. The more the fabric is painted and printed, the greater the complexity and surface interest.

Both her fabrics and her dye recipes are constantly evolving—consequently, her work reflects the process-oriented nature of her thinking. The elegant pieced coats and jackets sewn from her vibrant fabrics have an Asian overtone, and she acknowledges her lifelong appreciation of the Japanese aesthetic and culture.

Gienger believes that her creative work is linked to the spiritual, and she acknowledges the mystical and the mysterious as a part of her process. She reflects on this part of her life: "It's so important to acknowledge the spirit in everything. This allows you to be in the moment and enjoy the work to be done—all the little activities that you have to do to accomplish a huge goal. You have to be willing to walk barefoot through the fire."

Opposite page, left:

Ellen Gienger, *Kesa Tunic and Scarf*, 2000; silks; hand painted, printed, pieced, serged.

Photo: Polara Studios

Opposite page, right:

Ellen Gienger, *Kesa*, 2000; silks; hand painted and block printed, pieced, serged.

Photo: Polara Studios

Left:

Ellen Gienger, *Crinkle Chiffon Wrap*, 1999; silk chiffon; hand painted and block printed.

Photo: Jason Lee

SALLY
RYAN
FISHERS, INDIANA

"SINCE I BEGAN WORKING WITH FABRIC, MY WORK HAS BEEN ABOUT COLOR AND PATTERN. I HAVE CHOSEN TECHNIQUES THAT ARE GRAPHIC AND INTENTIONAL AND SHIED AWAY FROM RANDOM AND LESS CONTROLLED DYEING TECHNIQUES. WHILE I AM OFTEN IN AWE OF A PROCESS SUCH AS SHIBORI OR FABRIC MANIPULATION, I HAVE DESIRED THE SPECIFICITY OF DRAWING AS A BASIS FOR MY PATTERNS....DRAWING PATTERNS BY HAND LINKS MY HEART AND SPIRIT. IT LINKS MY CHILDHOOD URGES TO MARK. IT LINKS TO EVERY HUMAN YEARNING TO SPEAK WITH THE HAND."

Right:

Sally Ryan, *Fleurette Kimono Jacket*, 2001; rayon silk velvet; screenprinted with thickened dyes using split-font technique (color gradation blended on screen), handpainted with liquid dyes; silk trim.

Photo: Wilbur Montgomery
Model: Nicole Franklin

Opposite page:

Sally Ryan, *Acanthus Velvet Coat and Scarf*, 2000; rayon silk velvet; screenprinted with thickened dyes, handpainted with liquid dyes; silk trim.

Photo: Wilbur Montgomery
Model: Nicole Franklin

When Sally Ryan was a child
growing up outside Chicago, she studied drawing
and painting at the Art Institute of Chicago. This experience fed her early inclinations to become an artist—
she remembers vividly her visceral reaction to an exhibition of paintings by Matisse, whose joie de vivre and
love of color are compatible with Ryan's outlook on
life and work.

She went on to study fine arts at Indiana University in
Bloomington, and spent a year in Madrid, Spain, as a
part of her studies. She absorbed the wealth of historical painting that the Prado Museum had to offer.
During this year, she also took advantage of Spain's
readily available leather goods and created original
embellished vests and bags that she sold to boutiques
in Paris before she left Europe. This first "line" of work
was later sold in Marshall Field's department store in
Chicago.

Ryan temporarily denied herself a life as an artist
when she finished her degree in social work instead
of fine arts, and worked for four years at the welfare
department in Indianapolis, Indiana. Nevertheless, she
took up experimenting with batik in her basement. By
1978, she was dedicated to work in fiber and surface
design and developed into a well-known batik artist
and teacher.

After honing her skills in dyeing through batik, she
went on to explore other surface techniques that
included painting on silk, monoprinting, and discharging. By 1984, she was successfully making and
selling wearable art. Her interest in more complex
designs grew alongside her experimentation with new
techniques in an effort to keep her work fresh.

Today, her work is centered on a silk-screening technique that she developed and uses on velvet. Her
interest in calligraphic design—influenced in part by
historic textiles and universal symbols—has inspired
rich and ornate patterns that are compatible with her
method and the plush pile of her fabric.

To begin her process, the velvet is pulled taut over Japanese shinshi, or an assemblage of bamboo rods. Ryan then uses her silk-screening process to apply intricate patterns with thickened dyes. She employs several small, movable screens to apply the dye and develop the patterning for a particular garment. The heavy pile of the velvet retains most of the image while some of the dye develops a faded appearance that gives the fabric an aged appearance. Once the dyes are set, they serve as a resist, and she paints in other areas and the background. This method allows her to enhance the design that is established through printing.

She expresses the spiritual connection that she finds through her work:

The impetus for [my design] is the need to create pattern that expresses the human mind, hand, and spirit as a metaphor for a larger universal meaning. Pattern expresses life force and spirit. It represents energy—the universal essence.

Opposite page, left:
Sally Ryan, *Camelot Hooded Coat*, 2001; rayon silk velvet; screenprinted with thickened dyes, handpainted with liquid dyes; silk trim.
Photo: Wilbur Montgomery. Model: Nicole Franklin

Opposite page, right:
Sally Ryan, *Isabel Duster*, 2001; rayon silk velvet; screenprinted with thickened dyes using split-font technique (color gradation blended on screen), handpainted with liquid dyes; silk trim.
Photo: Wilbur Montgomery. Model: Nicole Franklin

Above:
Sally Ryan, *Nouveau Graphic Shawl and Scarf*, 2001; rayon silk velvet; discharge screenprinted; handpainted silk linings.
Photo: Wilbur Montgomery. Model: Nicole Franklin

Right:
Sally Ryan, *Fiori Long-Banded Coat*, 1999; rayon silk velvet; screenprinted with thickened dyes using split-font technique (color gradation blended on screen), handpainted with liquid dyes.
Photo: Wilbur Montgomery. Model: Nicole Franklin

PEGGOTTY CHRISTENSEN
PHOENIX, ARIZONA

"MY DESIGNS HAVE ALWAYS BEEN INFLUENCED BY NATURE AND ART (EVERYTHING FROM ANCIENT POTTERY AND JEWELRY TO DESIGNS ON BED SHEETS)....I HAVE AN IDEA OF WHAT I'M GOING TO MAKE AND, IN MOST CASES, HAVE THE PIECES OF THE PATTERN DRAWN OUT ON THE FABRIC. I DECIDE WHICH DESIGN ELEMENTS I WANT TO USE, OR HOW I WANT THE FINISHED PIECE TO LOOK, AND JUST BEGIN. MANY TIMES MY INSPIRATION COMES FROM ISOLATING SMALL AREAS OF WHAT I'VE ALREADY PAINTED AND LOOKING AT THE WAY COLORS BLEND TO CREATE NEW ONES."

Above:
Peggotty Christensen, *Spirals Coat*, 1998; silk/rayon velvet; devoré, hand painted with fiber-reactive dyes.
Photo: Bruce Talbot. Model: Tanya Barnes-Matt

Right:
Peggotty Christensen, *Kimono*, 2000; silk/rayon velvet; devoré, hand painted with fiber-reactive dyes.
Photo: Bruce Talbot. Model: Tanya Barnes-Matt

Opposite page:
Peggotty Christensen, *Windowpanes*, 1998; silk/rayon velvet; devoré, hand painted with fiber-reactive dyes.
Photo: Bruce Talbot. Model: Tanya Barnes-Matt

Her shift from metal to fabric about 15 years ago began with painting T-shirts, leggings, and dresses. Nevertheless, her interest in color and design was always the primary impetus for the work. "What I really wanted to do was paint the beautiful and bright clear colors I had seen on the silk," she says of her early trial-and-error process.

Created improvisationally with intuitive movements of the brush, her surfaces leave evidence of the mark of her hand in each finished piece. She begins the painting of her silks with fiber-reactive dyes by stretching white silk on a horizontal wooden frame. The outline of her simple garment patterns, blocked off with resist, serve as boundaries within which to paint her designs. Using sponge and natural bristle brushes, she blends the background colors before adding patterned designs on top.

Conceiving each segment of the garment as if it is a separate painting, her goal is to compose independent and strong compositions within the framework of each piece. After the silk is painted, she dries it before rolling and steaming it to lend the cloth a fine sheen. Excess dye is washed from the silk, and the pieces are then cut out and transformed into sleeves, flowing backs, or other parts of her kimono-like jackets and coats.

Peggotty Christensen first became intrigued with the possibilities of painting silk after seeing handpainted garments in Hawaii. After successfully making jewelry for many years, she was ready to try something new. She saw no reason why she couldn't create handpainted clothing, and she dove into the process of learning about silk painting through study and experimentation. Through what she describes as a "long process" to get where she is today, her work reflects the dedication of her years of exploration.

In a workshop that she took during 1995, she learned about devoré (chemical burnout of fabric)—a process which now defines a large portion of her work. By creating similar freeform designs on silk/rayon velvet, satin and crepe, silk/linen, and linen/polyester, she has broadened her field of possibilities. Working an average of 10 hours a day, seven days a week, Christensen enthusiastically pursues her artistry—out of excitement for the work that unceasingly compells her.

Opposite page:

Peggotty Christensen, *Jacket* **(detail), 2000; silk/rayon velvet; devoré, hand painted with fiber-reactive dyes.**

Photo: Bruce Talbot. Model: Tanya Barnes-Matt

Left:

Peggotty Christensen, *Dress and Triangle Scarf,* **2000; silk/rayon velvet; devoré, hand painted with fiber-reactive dyes.**

Photo: Bruce Talbot. Model: Tanya Barnes-Matt

Above:

Peggotty Christensen, *Dress and Scarf,* **2000; silk/rayon velvet; devoré, hand painted with fiber-reactive dyes.**

Photo: Bruce Talbot. Model: Tanya Barnes-Matt

NICK CAVE

"MY DESIGNS FOR CLOTHING HAVE ALWAYS BEEN SIMPLE. THE MOST IMPORTANT THING IS THAT MY CLOTHING HAS A POINT OF VIEW...THAT WHEN YOU VIEW THEM YOU START TO INVESTIGATE THE SMALL DETAILS IN THE CONSTRUCTION AS WELL AS RICHNESS AND THE MANIPULATION OF FABRICS. THE TECHNIQUES USED IN DEVELOPING MY FABRICS COME FROM MY SOLID BACKGROUND AS A PRINTER. I HAVE ALWAYS TREATED MY CLOTH AS A CANVAS, AND I LET IT EVOLVE AS I OPEN MYSELF UP TO THE PROCESS."

Opposite page, left:
Nick Cave, *Sound Suit*, 2001; crocheted and pieced afghan, sisal hemp, sequins.
Model: Nick Cave

Opposite page, right:
Nick Cave, Untitled; silks and microfiber fabrics; layered separates.
Photo: Nick Cave

Left:
Nick Cave, Untitled, 1998; silk, organza, cotton, linen, indigo; handpainted jacket.
Photo: Nick Cave

Nick Cave has been called
many things—an artist, an academician, a designer, a dancer, a performance artist, a sculptor. His multimedia/multi-dimensional approach to his art reflects the direct way in which he responds to his own personal history, and his need to stretch conventional boundaries. Cave says that he strives to create meaning in his work that "makes a difference in the lives of individuals."

Cave grew up in Missouri where he was encouraged by his family to explore his many interests that ranged from quilting to modern dance. He went on to earn his

B.F.A. at the Kansas City Art Institute in Missouri and his M.A. at the Cranbrook Academy of Art in Michigan. During 1989, he moved to Chicago to teach in the Fiber and Material Studies Department, where he taught until 1993. Today he is back at the school full time, teaching in the Fashion Department.

During the early 1990s, he used the artistic language of dance combined with elaborate costume to create a series that he named *Sound Suits*—works created to be used in both performance and for contemplation as art objects. The suits often incorporate discarded debri scavenged from his urban environment or thrift stores—bottle caps, sticks, feathers, crocheted fabrics—all recontextualized and reassembled into body coverings that somehow balance rarefied elegance and visceral awareness. When Cave dons one of the suits and moves to music, it creates its own idiosyncratic noise that adds to the mystery and dimensionality of the experience.

In the early 1990s when Cave was teaching at the Art Institute, designer Jeffrey Roberts attended a lecture that he presented about his performance work. After initial conversations, they were both drawn to the possibilities of collaborating with one another. These talks led to their conceptualization of a partnership to form Robave, Inc., a company that engages both of their talents and energies to create one-of-a-kind or limited edition handpainted clothing. Roberts and Cave spent close to three years in the planning stages for the company, debating both practical and ethical considerations of making clothing with extremely high standards that doesn't conform to a trendy market.

During 2001, Cave and Roberts purchased a four-story building in Chicago to serve as a studio and loft. They are in the concept-stage for new developments within the original concept of Robave, while Cave is concentrating on the creation of a new series of *Sound Suits* that he hopes to show in museums and use in performance around the world.

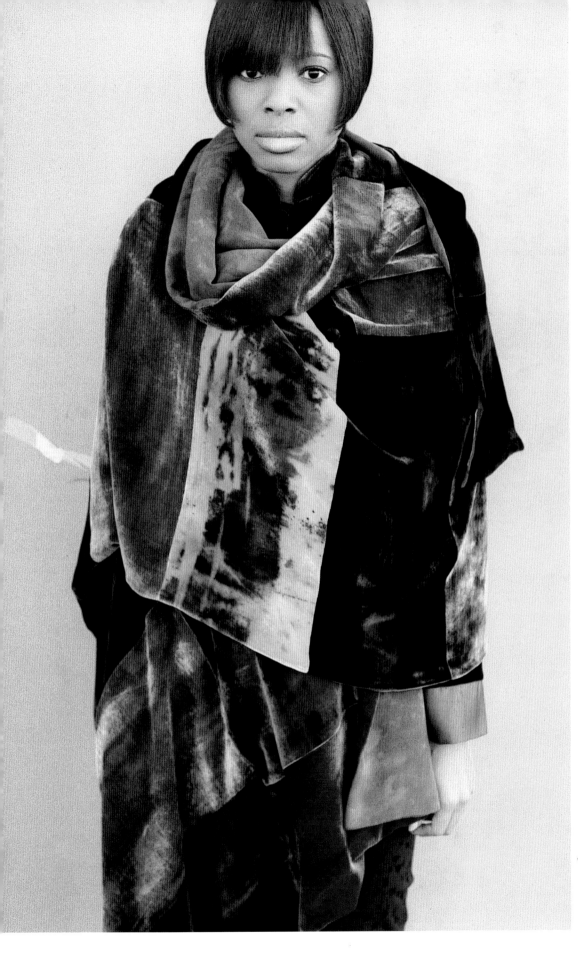

Opposite page, left:
Nick Cave, Untitled, 1997; silk; handpainted; organza jacket.
Photo: Nick Cave

Opposite page, right:
Nick Cave, Untitled, 1998; silk, constructed jacket; silk, dress.
Photo: Nick Cave

Left:
Nick Cave, Untitled, 1996; silk, velvet; handpainted, patched wrap.
Photo: Nick Cave

MICHELLE MARCUSE

PHILADELPHIA, PENNSYLVANIA

"A SPARKING OF THE CREATIVE PROCESS CAN INVOLVE LOOKING AT SOMETHING THAT MIGHT BE CONSIDERED COMMON IN DAILY USE, BUT SEEING AN ASPECT OF IT QUITE DIFFERENTLY. IT COULD MEAN PUTTING ON A GARMENT UPSIDE DOWN AND BACK TO FRONT. IT MEANS SEEING IN A WAY THAT IS DIFFERENT TO THE NORMAL WAY OF LOOKING....THAT OBJECT TRANSCENDS ITS CATEGORY/LABEL AND SUDDENLY HAS HUGE POTENTIAL IN WAYS THAT MIGHT NOT HAVE BEEN IMAGINED BEFORE...WHATEVER IT IS, THERE IS A WAY OF LOOKING AS IF IT IS FOR THE FIRST TIME."

Left:
Michelle Marcuse, Untitled, 1999-2000; painted silk organza.
Photo: Lindy Powers

Opposite page, left:
Michelle Marcuse, Untitled, 1999-2000; painted silk organza.
Photo: Lindy Powers

Opposite page, right:
Michelle Marcuse, Untitled, 1999-2000; painted silk organza.
Photo: Lindy Powers

The exploration of textile arts
is only part of Michelle Marcuse's artistic evolution. When she was around 20 years old, she chose to study textiles because it felt safer to her than getting a degree in art. She knew that she wanted to make a living doing creative work, but selected an "art-related field" rather than becoming a painter or sculptor.

Her search led her back to school to study painting, printmaking, and sculpture at the University of Cape Town in South Africa followed by painting at Tyler School of Art near Philadelphia. As she describes this process of learning about her subject as well as herself she says, "it was only years later that I decided to go with what was in me and nurture it...I am a very later developer...it makes me smile each time I do a full circle and come back to what originally sparked me."

One senses from talking to her that she doesn't see her life as a series of steps, but as relationships of the parts to the whole. Trying to make life conform to a linear, planned sequence that so many of us strive for doesn't work for her. She moves in an improvisational fashion—preferring not to be "intentional" in her work—answering to feelings that call her to the next stage.

The fresh originality of her work in painted silks and manipulated stitched fabric is a result of responding to her instincts without thinking about an audience. She has successfully sold her work for a number of years through prestigious craft shows, but recently found the business aspect of making clothing to sell too limiting.

Her current fascination is with encaustic painting, which she teaches through workshops around the country. She enjoys the exchange of teaching, and the money provides her with time be experimental with cloth and other media without the pressure of creating to sell. She prefers to keep her mind on the moment, defining her future as little as possible in order to stay open to new possibilties. Her courage to do this is inspiring in a commercially driven world that often promotes the possibility of scarcity as a tactic of manipulation. She shares what she has learned about letting go:

It is my belief from my experience that if I don't operate from fear and allow things to manifest and pay attention to the creation, that things happen naturally. Of course, my interaction with what is happening helps define the resulting work. I hardly ever keep a notebook, and if I do, very rarely refer back to it. I find that if I have to start creating after being away for a while, sometimes it is overwhelming. I have learned to either start with what I am comfortable with or where I left off last....And if I am ever reluctant to go and start work because I don't know where I am going, I know that the process is just 'walk up there [to the studio] and start.'

Opposite page:
Michelle Marcuse, Untitled, 1998; painted black organza, straight-stitched rows with circular stitched collar.
Photo: Jack Ramsdale

Right:
Michelle Marcuse, Untitled, 1996; organza; pin-tucked and painted with thickened fiber-reactive paint, shibori-wrapped for texture.
Photo: Lindy Powers

ALEXIS ABRAMS

LOS ANGELES, CALIFORNIA

"I REMEMBER BEING STRUCK BY THE REGRETTABLE TRUTH OF WRITER ELLEN DISSANAYAKE'S ASSERTION THAT WE LIVE IN 'A SOCIETY THAT DEVALUES MAKING.' I'D HAVE TO SAY I'VE NEVER FELT IN TUNE WITH THAT VALUE SYSTEM. FROM THE TIME I LEARNED TO SEW AND COOK BY WATCHING MY MOTHER, I'VE ALWAYS ENJOYED THE PROCESS OF MAKING THINGS AT LEAST AS MUCH AS HAVING THE FINAL PRODUCTS. IT'S REALLY PLEASURABLE FOR ME, NOW, TO TAKE A PIECE OF WHITE SILK AND SLOWLY TRANSFORM IT INTO SHEETS OF COLOR, ASSORTED MOSAICLIKE SHAPES, AND, FINALLY, A UNIQUE AND USEFUL GARMENT."

Right:
Alexis Abrams, *Shell Dress and Jacket*, 2001; silk crepe; painted (dress), silk chiffon; painted (jacket).
Photo: Barry Abrams. Model: Alexis Abrams

Opposite page:
Alexis Abrams, *Byzantine Jacket #5*, 1999; silk crepe; painted, block printed, pieced; lined with silk crepe.
Photo: Barry Abrams. Model: Alexis Abrams

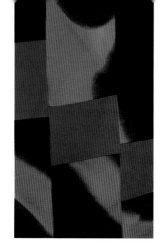

A matter of practicality first
influenced Alexis Abrams' move from making paintings
for the wall to creating paintings for the body. After she
and her husband moved to Los Angeles from New
England in the late 1970s, they spent many afternoons
exploring the California terrain—beaches, mountains,
and deserts—that ultimately inspired her to make
large, abstract three-dimensional wall pieces. During the
same period, she began to work for a clothing designer
as a seamstress and cutter.

As it turned out, the wall pieces were "too delicate and
unwieldy" to be easily shipped or stored—making it difficult for Abrams to show and promote her work. Working
as a seamstress shifted her mind to clothing, and she
began to think about it as a possible canvas for her
abstract forms. She began applying the same dyes and
ideas that she had used on her wall pieces to jackets.

Following a trip to Sante Fe in the late 1980s, where
she was inspired by seeing artists making a living from
their artwork, she decided to try to make a living creating art-to-wear. Looking back, she credits her jewelry
teacher, Jill Slosburg, at the Massachusetts College of

Art in Boston, with making the "distinction...between
fine art and functional art...seem irrelevant." Abrams
has never regretted her decision to make art in the form
of clothing, noting that the field's intrinsic "combination
of color and fabric combined with the pleasures and
challenges of design and construction" suit her well.

Abrams does all of her own dye-painting, cutting, and
sewing, which allows her the opportunity to monitor and
adjust each step in the process. A color theme or combination is usually her point of departure inspired by visits
to museums, books of paintings, nature, or most anything in her environment. After playing around with color
samples, she begins work on white silk stretched over a
large horizontal wooden frame. Using a watercolor technique, she paints the fabric with various shades of fabric
dyes that she has mixed. After the fabric dries, it is
steamed to permanently set the dyes before washing
and drying. At this point, she may choose to add strokes
of gold paint or blockprint images in gold. To create the
pieced jackets, she tears the fabric into strips and sews
them together into larger pieces that are then cut out as
garment pieces and juxtaposed with solid fabrics.

The compelling nature of her painted cloth results from
her ability to focus on a few elements arrived at by
repeating and working out a theme. She notes that she
has "always admired Monet's *Haystacks* and *Water
Lilies* and Rothko's color meditations." A series of variations "gives the original idea the space and time to
grow from one piece to another," she continues. She
admires clothing that has "an element of understate-
ment," and her work reflects this quality while assert-
ing itself through sophisticated color combinations and
elegant design.

Right:
**Alexis Abrams, *Red
Square Coat*, 2001;
silk crepe;
painted, pieced; lined
with painted silk crepe.**
Photo: Barry Abrams
Model: Alexis Abrams

Opposite page:
**Alexis Abrams,
Byzantine Coat #12,
1999; silk crepe;
painted, block printed,
pieced; lined
with silk crepe.**
Photo: Barry Abrams
Model: Alexis Abrams

CYNTHIA WAYNE GAFFIELD

FARMINGTON HILLS, MICHIGAN

"I BEGIN WITH A BLANK, WHITE CANVAS OF TEXTURED SILK. I STRETCH THE SILK OVER A FRAME AND HAND PAINT THE FABRIC USING FIBER-REACTIVE DYES. THESE DYES HAVE THE CONSISTENCY OF WATER COLORS AND CHEMICALLY BOND WITH THE SILK, WHICH DYES THE ENTIRE PIECE, AS OPPOSED TO THE SURFACE ALONE. THE FABRIC IS DRIED, STEAM-SET FOR COLOR PERMANENCE, RINSED, WASHED, AND THEN DRIED AGAIN. IT IS THEN READY TO BE CUT AND SEWN. BECAUSE EACH LENGTH OF FABRIC IS DISTINCT AND INDIVIDUAL, I CHOOSE SPECIFICALLY INTERESTING AREAS WHEN CUTTING THE PATTERN FOR DIFFERENT PARTS OF THE GARMENT. SEMI-PRECIOUS BEADS AND APPLIQUÉS ARE APPLIED DURING THE FINISHING STAGE OF CREATION."

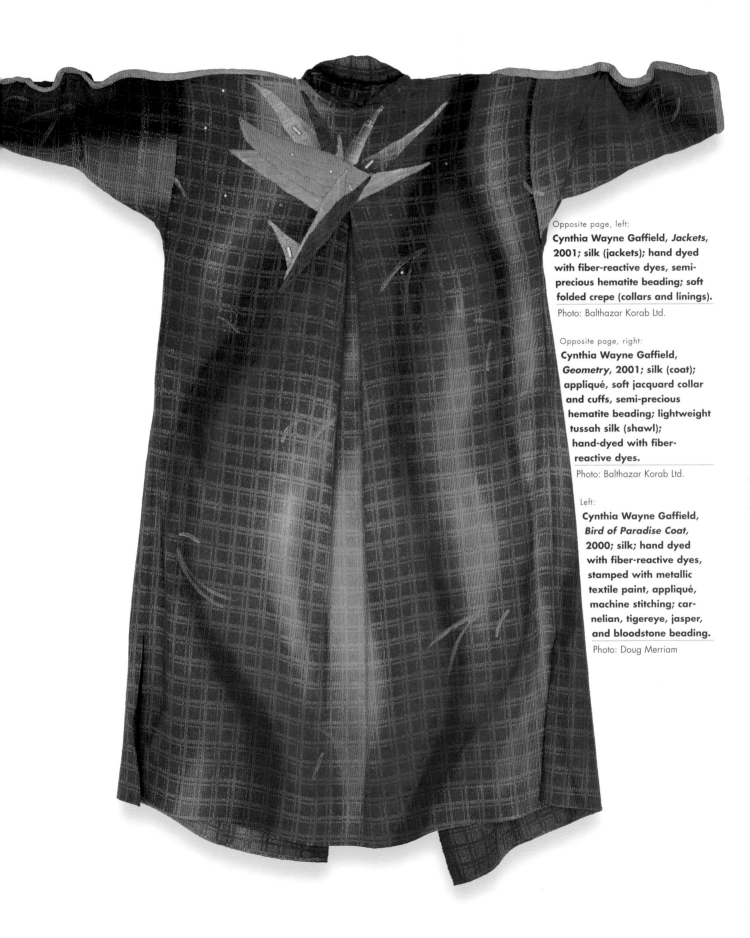

Opposite page, left:
Cynthia Wayne Gaffield, *Jackets*, 2001; silk (jackets); hand dyed with fiber-reactive dyes, semi-precious hematite beading; soft folded crepe (collars and linings).
Photo: Balthazar Korab Ltd.

Opposite page, right:
Cynthia Wayne Gaffield, *Geometry*, 2001; silk (coat); appliqué, soft jacquard collar and cuffs, semi-precious hematite beading; lightweight tussah silk (shawl); hand-dyed with fiber-reactive dyes.
Photo: Balthazar Korab Ltd.

Left:
Cynthia Wayne Gaffield, *Bird of Paradise Coat*, 2000; silk; hand dyed with fiber-reactive dyes, stamped with metallic textile paint, appliqué, machine stitching; carnelian, tigereye, jasper, and bloodstone beading.
Photo: Doug Merriam

When Cynthia Gaffield was in middle school, her art teacher covered the walls of the classroom and allowed her and others to "throw paint" without consequences—a liberating experience that Gaffield still recalls. Later in life, she found her way into graphic design and worked for 15 years in the field before she admitted to herself that she had to find a "more rewarding outlet" for her creativity. During her search, she tried making a line of purses, but the fit wasn't exactly right for her. Later, she took a silk painting workshop and was "immediately hooked"— not only on the technique but the textural possibilities of the fabric. During the early 1980s, she found that there was a market for her painted silks, and she felt confident that she could make a living doing what she loved. In 1983, she stopped working as a graphic designer and became a fiber artist.

Her passion for the painted cloth led her to carve out a niche in the fiber world that is recognizably her own. The flowing coats, jackets, and scarves that she creates allow the pattern and color of her paintings on fabric to be clearly seen. Beginning with coarse, raw silk that is woven with various finishes to fit her specifications, she paints the fabric with color fields of dye that are allowed to interact, bleed into one another, and produce variations of color. The process often involves stepping back before adding more rich, saturated color. As the cloth dries, the interaction of color continues to evolve, leading to some unpredictable results in the final cloth.

She adds repeated motifs to the surface of her dyed cloth with hand-carved stamps and metallic textile pigment. Her visual vocabulary is often inspired by naturally occuring patterns found in "things as simple as pebbles, pine needles, and leaves or as complex as the intricate honeycomb patterns of a beehive." An avid gardener who spends a lot of time outdoors, her love of patterning extends into this sphere where she creates small "installations" of found objects in her garden.

Along with the work that she is so passionate about, she has found a rich community of fellow artists,

gallery owners, and clients. "I have a couple of friends, and they know who they are, who push and inspire me," she reflects. "They believe that there is no limit to my abilities, and their support encourages me to aim higher."

PATRICIA ELMES FARLEY

PITTSBURGH, PENNSYLVANIA

"I WORK BEST WHEN I WORK QUICKLY AND DON'T LET THE LEFT BRAIN TAKE OVER. WHETHER I'M WAXING OR PAINTING OR PIECING [THE FABRIC], MY BEST WORK ALWAYS HAPPENS SPONTANEOUSLY. I RARELY SKETCH ANYTHING AHEAD OF TIME, NEEDING THE ACTUAL MATERIALS AND TOOLS IN MY HAND IN ORDER TO CREATE....I FIND A BALANCE BETWEEN DOING THE REPETITIVE WORK, WHICH IS VERY MEDITATIVE FOR ME, AND THE NEW, EXCITING AND ALWAYS A LITTLE SCARY CHALLENGE OF EXPLORING A NEW PROCESS."

Left:
Patricia Elmes Farley, *Flame Great Shirt,* **2000;** linen; batiked using wax and fiber-reactive dyes.

Opposite page:
Patricia Elmes Farley, *Midnight Great Shirt,* **2000;** linen; batiked using wax and fiber-reactive dyes.

She draws abstract lines and shapes with the hot wax that she applies with a tjanting tool or a brush.

After applying the wax, she mixes her dyes and applies them to the fabric with a foam brush. She says that she "used to fill in motifs and stay in the lines" but now allows the dye "go all sorts of places," creating an improvisational look of colors that have blended and washed over one another.

After the first layer is finished, she applies a second layer of pattern and color. In addition to batik, she uses textile inks, stamps that she designs, prints from found objects, discharging, and silk-screening. She has a strong interest in collage that she is able to explore through the use of layering and stamping. After applying the designs, the fabric must be washed at least twice, then dry-cleaned to thoroughly remove all of the wax.

Her method of painting directly on the cloth is intuitive and process-oriented. It also allows her to work quickly, "before the left brain takes over," as she says. She

As a weaver, Patricia Farley was always fascinated by the layering of colored yarns to create the warp and the weft of the cloth. About nine years ago, she began to translate this fascination into surface design using batik. (Simply put, the wax that serves as a resist for the dye in traditional batik forms lines for containing the colorful shapes that she paints.)

The fabrics that she uses vary: textured linen woven in Poland, linen gauze woven in Belgium, cottons from Peru and the United States, or silks from China and India. She begins by stretching the white fabric on a frame, usually working on 5 to 8 yards at a time.

designs all of her clothing and cuts some of the pieces before they are passed on to others to sew together. The production work that she produces has been her most profitable, but she also produces limited edition and one-of-a-kind pieces. She divides her work as follows: The production pieces are generally batiked or printed all over, the limited edition works have some degree of piecing, and the one-of-a-kind creations are very elaborately pieced and quilted. In other words, there is a direct correlation between how much time is spent on a piece and how she categorizes it.

The 12-hour days that she spends in her large studio in Pittsburgh's Strip District, working alongside assistants, are balanced by her yearly retreat from August until October to Chincoteague Island, located off the coast of Virginia. There she is able to work on new ideas and recover, away from the hectic pace of her urban studio. She acknowledges her need for this balance in her life that is ultimately reflected in her designs.

The vibrant colors and abstract shapes of her charismatic work are inspired by a host of influences that she randomly lists: motifs from the 1950s, the paintings and drawings of Joan Miro, graffiti, gradations of color found in the environment of the beach and marsh, the regular grid of a traditional quilt, the contemporary quilts of Nancy Crow, waves and curves and roundness, smooth beach stones, visionary art, food, African textiles, mud cloth, her husband's gardens, and clotheslines.

Opposite page, left:
Patricia Elmes Farley, *Star Jacket,* **1999; linen; batiked, silk screened, printed, discharged, dyed.**

Opposite page, right:
Patricia Elmes Farley, *Meadow City Jacket,* **1999; linen/cotton blend; batiked, quilted, edged in bias strip; reversible.**

Right:
Patricia Elmes Farley, *Down To The Sea,* **2000; linen; dyed, batiked, discharged, printed, pieced.**

DEBORAH
HIRD
KALISPELL, MONTANA

"I LOVE DOING SURFACE DESIGN WORK. I FIND IT AN ABSOLUTE JOY TO 'PLAY.' I LOVE THE IMMEDIACY OF THE WORK. I AM CONSTANTLY BEING LED FROM ONE DESIGN TO ANOTHER, ONE INSPIRES THE NEXT....CURRENTLY I AM IMMERSED IN LAYERING DESIGNS. I LOVE THE PLAY OF STRONG GEOMETRIC SHAPES OVERLAID WITH ORGANIC IMAGES. I UTILIZE EVERYTHING I FIND THAT WILL TAKE ME WHERE I WANT TO GO."

Opposite page, left:
Deborah Hird, *Gameboard Jacket, Scarf and Top,* 2000; rayon bouclé; discharged.
Photo: John Cooper. Stylist: Peter Brown. Model: Julie Zeger
Courtesy of Bellagio; Asheville, North Carolina

Opposite page, right:
Deborah Hird, *Brocade Century Coat,* 2000; rayon bouclé; hand painted, hand-cut and manipulated stencils.
Photo: John Cooper. Stylist: Peter Brown. Model: Julie Zeger
Courtesy of Bellagio; Asheville, North Carolina

Above, left:
Deborah Hird, *Overlay Fringed Coat,* 1999; rayon bouclé; hand painted.
Photo: John Cooper. Stylist: Peter Brown. Model: Julie Zeger
Courtesy of Dream Weaver Gallery; Sarasota, Florida

Above right:
Deborah Hird, *Brocade Century Coat,* 2000; rayon bouclé; hand painted, hand-cut and manipulated stencils.
Photo: John Cooper. Stylist: Peter Brown. Model: Julie Zeger
Courtesy of Bellagio; Asheville, North Carolina

Deborah Hird finds inspiration for her work everywhere. She once found a small button in New York that ignited her idea for a whole series of painted jackets and coats. She sometimes has trouble keeping up with the ideas that flood her mind, so she makes notes and sketches when the muse strikes in earnest, saving them for later.

Many of her pieces bear a striking grid pattern orginally inspired by a floor grate from her dining room. After thinking about the possibilities of the grate, she discovered some recycled scrap metal grates that had been used by a sculptor and began using them as stencils.

Today, she still uses the grates to create exciting designs on her fabric. In this process, the grids are weighted down on the fabric before she sprays on bottled color from various angles to create results that are always fresh and slightly out of her control. She often adds paint to the surface of the grid and then presses it onto the surface of the fabric to create more unpredictable effects. To create other shapes, she cuts out pieces of polyester film to use as masks and paints around them on the fabric. Also in her bag of techniques is the shibori-resist dye technique to discharge the fabric in a number of ways and with various materials.

Before she is able to "play" at her surface design, her unique fabrics are made from yarns that she designs—made to her specifications by a mill in California to assure the texture and drape that she wants. The yarn is then dyed in Pennsylvania, following her dictates of palette, before being woven into simple weave structures.

Until about 20 years ago, Hird worked as a weaver who wove wall hangings. Her thinking about wearable art began as she sat at the loom painting her warps. She envisioned a large orchid wrapped around a coat, made her first piece of wearable art, and soon afterward met a weaver who made clothing who influenced her to sell woven garments. The response to her work was so positive that she changed the focus of her work to wearable art.

Her career in wearables gained momentum, and she was eventually invited to show at the prestigious American Craft Council show in Baltimore, Maryland. Only two days before the show, she was involved in a head-on car accident that redirected her life again. The damage to her neck and shoulder from the crash meant she could no longer position herself over a loom, painting detailed warps with a brush.

She abandoned surface design and began doing production work with the assistance of other weavers. Eventually, she ended up in a large studio overlooking the Rockies to provide the space needed for the many steps of her process—from color design of yarns to shipping and receiving.

Today, she is able to concentrate on the conceptual part of her work—the painting and embellishment of her surfaces inspired by her adventuresome and inquisitive spirit.

Left:
**Deborah Hird, *Medallion Coat*, 2000;
rayon bouclé; handpainted.**
Photo: John Cooper. Stylist: Peter Brown. Model: Julie Zeger

Right:
**Deborah Hird, *Boa Suit*, 1999; rayon bouclé;
handwoven, discharged.**
Photo: John Cooper. Stylist: Peter Brown. Model: Julie Zeger
Courtesy of Bellagio; Asheville, North Carolina

MARY JAEGER
NEW YORK, NEW YORK

"I AM MOTIVATED BY THE DESIRE TO LEARN AND CHANGE....MY REAL PASSION LIES IN THE STUDY OF 'TRADITIONAL' DYEING AND SURFACE EMBELLISHMENT TECHNIQUES LIKE JAPANESE TEGAKI YUZEN, SHIBORI, TSUTSUGAMI (JAPANESE FINGERNAIL WEAVING), INDONESIAN TULIS BATIK, AND INTRICATE EMBROIDERY AND BEADING WORK LIKE THAT DONE IN CHINA, JAPAN, OR MOROCCO. I APPRECIATE THE CRAFTSMANSHIP, TECHNIQUE, DESIGNS AND UTILITARIAN FOCUS OF ANTIQUE TEXTILE PIECES, ACCESSORIES, AND GARMENTS. MANY OF THESE TECHNIQUES ARE DISAPPEARING AS CULTURES CHANGE AND TECHNOLOGY IS INTRODUCED. THE CHALLENGE OF DESIGNING MY COLLECTIONS IS TO MAINTAIN THE ARTISTIC INTEGRITY OF THE TEXTILE USING HANDS-ON TECHNIQUES, YET MODERNIZE THE DESIGN AND FUNCTION."

Right:
Mary Jaeger, *Kimono Mosaic Wrap: Momoji and Coral Shibori*, 2001; vintage kimono pieces contrasted with contemporary silks; reversible with comparable pattern on each side.
Photo: Stuart Liben. Model: Saori Tanaka.

Opposite page:
Mary Jaeger, *Himalayan Long Shawl*, 2001; wool, silk, nylon blend; limited edition: 1/2.
Photo: Stuart Liben. Model: Saori Tanaka.

Influenced by centuries-old techniques, Mary Jaeger's work supplies an innovative bridge between the distant past and the yet-to-be future. Fusing the energies innate to Western innovation and Eastern mastery of process, she creates bodies of work that echo her creative desires and changing interests. She has cultivated her own aesthetic through processes that are used as tools for the expression of her ideas.

After studies in apparel, textiles, and related arts at the University of Wisconsin in Madison, The University of Notre Dame in Indiana, and The Fashion Institute of Technology in New York, she pursued the study of traditional textile techniques in Japan. There she learned to think of her work in textiles as an art form. Her academic studies in Kyoto during the 1980s centered on hand painting on silk (direct and resist dye applications) as well as surface embellishments such as beading and embroidery. The discipline acquired through learning textile techniques such as *tegaki yuzen*, that involves around 15 different steps to create finely-shaded painterly scenes on silk, aided her road to success as an artist and businessperson.

After two years of formal schooling in Japan, she was invited to work with a kimono company called Koei Kogei to design a collection of western-styled clothing using a traditional Japanese textile design method. Her work gained her acclaim which lent her opportunities to design important collections in Japan and Europe over the next few years.

After her years abroad, she longed to return to the United States. She sold her designs in gallery and trunk shows across the country and marketed her work with the help of an agent. Eventually, she established a design studio in New York City, where she still works today. In 1998, she and her husband collaborated in the process of opening a store to house her creations in NoLIta (North of Little Italy), an area just east of Soho in New York. Jaeger notes that she enjoys the "challenge

and flexibility" of having her own retail business. She uses the internet as a resource for reaching a global audience, while her store serves as a place to exhibit her collection and educate patrons about textile processes.

Through the years, Jaeger's collections have engaged a "cross-culture blending of techniques, fabrics, and colors," which she acknowledges as the most satisfying aspect of her work. Her most recent work with wool incorporates a texturing technique that she considers to be her signature look. From this raw material, she sculpts three-dimensional pieces by stitching a series of geometrically-placed tucks into the flat fabric. "The resulting textiles resemble topographic landscapes and encourage the wearer to wrap the shawls and capes in a multitude of ways, pushing the mountainous dimples in and out, creating their own look," she explains. Jaeger feels that "the possibilities for this surface texturing are limitless."

As she hits her creative stride in the diverse world of the 21st century, Jaeger seems to have learned how to successfully meet the market on her own terms—driven by the fuel of years of preparation, research, discipline, and innovation.

Left:
Mary Jaeger, *Scandinavian Forest at Midnight*, 1995; crinkle silk; batik resist, hand painted.
Photo: Tom McInvale. Model: Sabrina Fassbinder

Opposite page, left:
Mary Jaeger, *Mondrian Network*, 2001; wool; hand tucked, detailed with cube hematite beading; silk charmeuse bias skirt.
Photo: Stuart Liben. Model: Saori Tanaka

Opposite page, right:
Mary Jaeger, *Kimono Mosaic Wrap: Spring Under the Sumptuary Laws*, 2001; vintage kimono pieces contrasted with contemporary silks, reversible with comparable pattern on each side.
Photo: Stuart Liben. Model: Saori Tanaka

THE FIBERARTS BOOK OF WEARABLE ART   **99**

CATHERINE
BACON
NOVATO, CALIFORNIA

"I CREATE FASHION WITH A COMMUNITY OF ARTISTS....I STRIVE TO PRODUCE CLOTHING THAT IS UNIQUE BUT WEARABLE, AND THAT INCORPORATES QUALITY OF CRAFTSMANSHIP AND ARTISTIC EXPRESSION ON MANY LEVELS AND FROM A VARIETY OF SOURCES....MY PROCESS, THEN, IS A COLLABORATIVE ONE, AN ARTISTIC MARRIAGE OF HARMONIOUS ELEMENTS....EACH SOURCE HAS A COLLABORATIVE PART TO PLAY IN THE EVOLUTION OF A COLLECTION....THUS, I SEE MYSELF AS A COLLAGE ARTIST, ASSEMBLING ELEMENTS AND MEDIA THAT I HAVE MODIFIED TO IMPROVE THE MARRIAGE."

Opposite page:

Catherine Bacon, *Nomads Collection*, 1995; rayon chenille coat and hat, hand loomed by Eliza Urszula. Brocade vest, flannel shirt, and accessory clothing of imported fabrics.

Photo: Susan Schelling. Makeup: Victor Hutchings
Hair: Dawn Sutti. Jewelry: Susan Green

Far left:

Catherine Bacon, *Water from The Elements Collection*, 2000; silk chiffon, silk georgette (short kimono); tassel top and narrow bias skirt. Textile printing by Denise Elke.

Photo: Susan Schelling

Left:

Catherine Bacon, *Asian Splendor Collection*, 2001; silk chiffon coat with textile design by Susan Avila. Chiffon shawl. French beaded shell fabric with custom dyed lining. Wide leg pants of Indian mirrored fabric.

Photo: Susan Schelling

Above:

Catherine Bacon, *Earth from The Elements Collection*, 2000; Italian velvet; silk screened (kimono); hand-beaded French fabric (shell and skirt).

Photo: Susan Schelling

Catherine Bacon is the first to admit that she doesn't fit into the "one-of-a-kind" hand-made wearable category. She is a designer who collaborates with others who make the fabrics and accessories that she assembles into singular and striking ensembles.

She layers fabrics, unusual color, and narrative references to create a rich but unified whole. The material for her pieces comes from many sources—for instance, she may work closely with a mill in Italy to produce a fabric and with another in France to acquire hand-beaded fabric. She works with an array of talented textile designers, fabric painters, knitters, and others who contribute the components that she brings together.

Bacon's themed collections conjure up a lot of words, but never ones that connote ordinary. Her fall 2001 collection centered on ancient Egypt, described in inviting, poetic language by Bacon's announcement of it as "a collection that explores the colors and symbols of mortal adornment on the pathway to the Divine." She describes the orchestration of her collections:

> My collections are driven by themes, rather than by one or two individual components, such as surface texture and color. While those are important parts of the whole for me, I attempt to create collections that work within a larger context. I research themes and symbols, studying their history and past cultural importance, to reach a greater understanding of their source's application and power.

Her work has been called ethereal and, for her, is infused with spiritual elements and sacred symbols. She believes that she is making a contribution to the world by connecting with the inherent beauty of the wearer. Her ability to do this has won her the attention of the famous, such as Ellen Burstyn, who commissioned her to create the handbeaded white gown that she wore to an Academy Awards ceremony.

This designer of sublime couture lives in an ordinary neighborhood in Novato, California—a suburb of San

Francisco—in a home with a converted studio garage. On a warm summer day, she interrupts a moment of thoughtful conversation about her work to speak affectionately to her newest associate, a standard poodle named Grace.

For her, it appears, the universal is found in everything from poodles to ancient symbols. This lively collaborator takes her work seriously, but not without maintaining the balance of seeing herself as a creative contributor to the whole.

Opposite page:
Catherine Bacon, *Asian Splendor Collection*, 2001; organza; handprinted by Valeri Clarke.
Photo: Susan Schelling

Right:
Catherine Bacon, *Mount Everest Coat from the Snow Leopard Collection*, 1999; silk and rayon velvet; fabric hand printed by Ed Krayer. Skirt and bell top of Italian fabric.
Photo: Susan Schelling. Makeup: Victor Hutchings.
Hair: Dawn Sutti. Jewelry: Susan Green

Below:
Catherine Bacon, *Tree of Life*, 2001; (motif inspired by Mariano Fortuny); devoré velvet mantle silkscreened by Valeri Clark. Narrow pant of Indian brocade. Beaded shell of fabric handbeaded in France. French custom color lining.
Photo: Susan Schelling.

LAURIE SCHAFER

SAN MARCOS, CALIFORNIA

"INITIALLY, I JUST DREW FANTASY GARMENTS AND SEWED FASHION. BUT AS MY KNOWLEDGE AND LOVE OF FINE FABRICS GREW, I WAS FRUSTRATED BECAUSE I EITHER COULD NOT FIND THE FABRIC OR COULD NOT AFFORD IT. SO I STARTED TO CREATE MY OWN LUXURIOUS COUTURE FABRICS....I FEEL THAT COUTURE IS A TRUE ART FORM. FABRIC IS MERELY A CANVAS...ARTWEAR AND COUTURE ARE TIMELESS; THEY DO NOT GO OUT OF STYLE."

Opposite page:
Laurie Schafer, *These Are Days We'll Remember*, 1994; silk dupioni; heavily appliquéd in silk dupioni and velvet; lined in silk dupioni with gold caligraphy by artist; quilted, couched, and wired collar.
Photo: Wayne Torberg

Right:
Laurie Schafer, *Midnight Kimono*, 1996; silk organza; kimono appliquéd with silk dupioni.
Photo: Warwick Greene

holdover from the previous generation of artists who looked at artwear as women's work." Nevertheless, she notes, as men became involved in the field, and more women became curators, the field was taken more seriously. She acknowledges that it might have been easier to make a living as a fashion designer, but she was compelled by her vision of creating work that expressed her individuality instead of the market.

Today, she has developed a distinctive technique and look that seem to play off her early interest in the color and pattern of the 1960s. Although her surfaces are sometimes mistaken for painted silk, she uses a time-consuming and precise method of appliquéing silk dupioni shapes, which have been pieced or dyed, onto her background "canvas" of organza, silk, or crushed velvet.

She rarely sketches out her ideas in detail, but begins with a basic garment shape in mind. Then she chooses the background fabric and the color scheme. On a very elaborate piece, she may use up to five colors of appliqué. After cutting out the pieces of her garment, she uses fusible webbing to hold the pieces in place, often layering more than one shape on top of another to create depth. Once the pieces are positioned, she uses an industrial sewing machine to sew the tight, intricate designs. She uses black thread to appliqué all of the pieces, creating what she calls a "stained glass effect." Her garments are highly finished in the tradition of couture; for instance, they are either lined or have French seams.

Schafer's luscious and boldly patterned coats and garments, replete with fanciful curlicues, play off one another in an open-ended, evolving manner. Shamelessly beautiful and joyous, they make no apologies for embracing a child's dreams of being an artist.

When Laurie Schafer was a
child, she loved to draw, paint, and sculpt—while her fantasies of making clothing were relegated to drawings and making paper dolls to wear her imaginary clothing. She saw the seasonal, ephemeral nature of fashion, and, in her mind, saw it as limiting for an artist. Nevetheless, she was a natural at making clothes, and made complete ensembles, including hats and purses, after learning to sew at age 11.

The 1960s rolled around and opened a new world for her. Art, fashion, and music collided in Pop, Op, the psychedelic. She was especially fond of the work of Peter Max. The lines blurred between art and fashion. Later, she studied costume design at the University of Minnesota, then began her career in art-to-wear—but not without feeling the frustration of not being accepted as an artist. She saw this attitude as "a chauvinistic

Opposite page:
**Laurie Schafer, *High Crossover Jacket*, 1996;
silk dupioni; appliquéd in silk dupioni.**
Photo: Warwick Greene

Above:
**Laurie Schafer, *Golden Kiss Kimono*, 2000; velvet,
sequins, silk dupioni; appliquéd with velvet.**
Photo: Tom Henderson. Model: Monica Moncrief

Left:
**Laurie Schafer, *Jacket and Madhatter*, 1996;
silk dupioni; appliquéd in silk dupioni.**
Photo: Warwick Greene

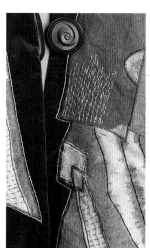

JANE
STEINSNYDER
PHILADELPHIA, PENNYSYLVANIA

"I BELIEVE IN THE TRANSFORMATION THAT OCCURS THROUGH CLOTHING AS I HAVE DIS-
COVERED IN MY STUDY OF THE CULTURES OF AFRICA, THE SOUTH PACIFIC, AND
INDONESIA. IN TRIBAL SOCIETY COSTUME IS AN INDICATOR OF RITUAL AND STATUS AND
CLEARLY DEFINES ONE'S ROLE IN THE COMMUNITY. IN OUR CONTEMPORARY SOCIETY
THERE IS AN EMPHASIS ON SAMENESS IN THE WAY WE DRESS, WITH LITTLE CHANGE FROM
EVERYDAY ACTIVITIES TO SPECIAL EVENT FUNCTIONS. MY INTEREST IN INTRODUCING
TRIBAL TEXTILES INTO THE CLOTHING I DESIGN IS TO CREATE A RICH SURFACE EMBEL-
LISHED WITH EMBROIDERY OR ORNAMENTS AS WELL AS TO SUGGEST A TRANSITION FROM
ONE CULTURE TO ANOTHER AND FROM COSTUME TO CLOTHING."

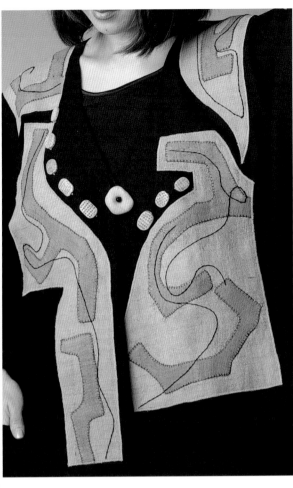

Opposite page:
**Jane Steinsnyder, *Jacket*, 2000;
silk broad cloth appliqué on nylon mesh.**
Photo: John Carlano. Model: Sung Hee

Left:
**Jane Steinsnyder, *Jacket* (detail), c. 1998; Kuba
textiles appliquéd on wool, hand embroidery, bead
ornamentation. (The button is stone and was part of a
necklace from the Dogon people of Mali, Africa.)**
Photo: John Carlano. Model: Sung Hee

Below:
**Jane Steinsnyder, *Jacket* (detail), 2000; Kuba textile
appliqué with hand embroidery on nylon mesh.**
Photo: John Carlano. Model: Sung Hee.

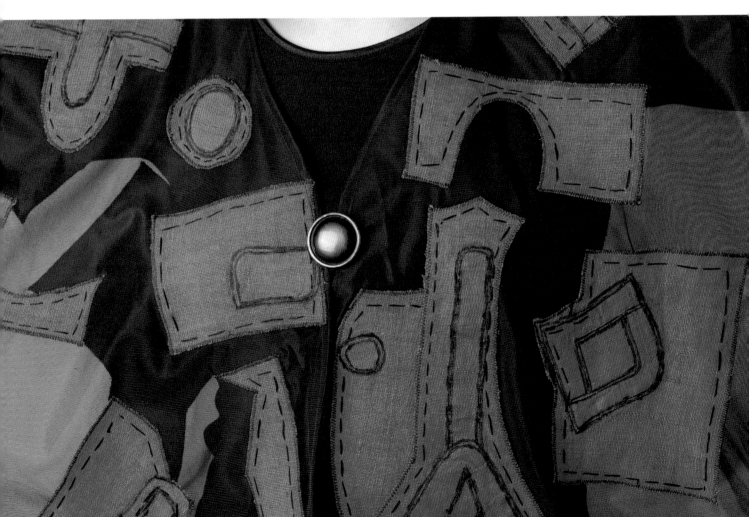

Jane Steinsnyder's art is a
metaphor for her life——it is a rich collage derived from
varied life experiences and knowledge brought together
into a pleasing whole. Looking at her life in hindsight,
influences and interests led her progressively to her work
in wearable art today.

She has always worked with or produced art in some
form. She studied at the Philadelphia College of Art
(now the University of the Arts) before going on to the
University of Miami in Florida, where she earned an
M.F.A. For 20 years, she taught drawing, painting, and
design at the college level. She maintained a studio for
her own work, participated in exhibitions, and curated
exhibitions of contemporary and tribal art at a college
gallery in Miami.

She returned to Philadelphia in the early 1980s, and
her interest in collage began to forecast the work that
she does today:

> When I moved back to Philadelphia, I began to do
> some drawings from nature which I cut and reassem-
> bled on large canvases to create a more abstract
> image. Gradually, I began to introduce fabric in these
> collages until the work became more a juxtaposition
> of textile shapes with a painted line superimposed.

For many years, she had also been collecting and dealing in African and South Pacific tribal textiles and sculpture, and decided to open a gallery on Pine Street in
Philadelphia when an opportunity presented itself.
Dubbed by one reporter as the "Gucci's of the Third
World"——filled with everything from Mali mudcloth
neckties to African headrests——the gallery also housed
a back room crammed with jackets, skirts, belts, and
tunics marketed under the Cassowary label. Some of the
garments were compilations designed by Steinsnyder
and a fashion designer, utilizing bits of damaged textiles
that were not salable. She combined segments of textiles from a variety of sources that ranged from Bolivian
weaves to antique wool rugs.

Since 1997, this interest in textiles and collage has evolved into the creation of her collections:

> I start with a few basic shapes of jackets, coats, and vests in linen, cotton, or wool fabrics. More recently, I began to experiment with transparency and used nylon mesh and silk organza as my background fabrics. On these canvases, I compose with shapes made of ethnic textiles, and then draw with an embroidered line before embellishing with beads, bones, buttons, and other ornaments.

The choices that Steinsnyder makes as she cuts, selects, and arranges shapes on fabric reflect her interest in abstract painting. She cites the works of Picasso, Matisse, de Kooning, Léger, and Krasner as those that stimulate her "thinking about form and how the elements of color, line, and composition can work for [her]."

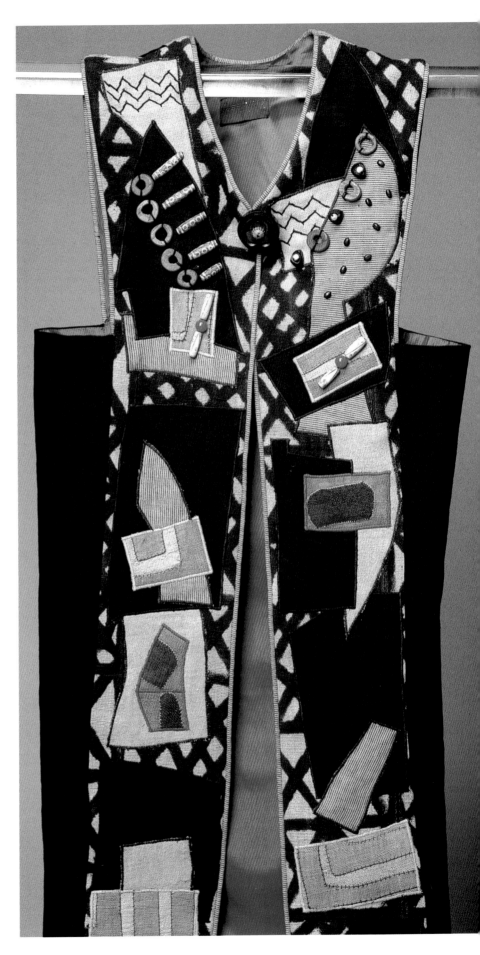

Opposite page:
Jane Steinsnyder, *Coat*, c. 1997; handwoven Bokolofini textile (mudcloth); appliquéd, bead ornaments.
Photo: Paternostro

Right:
Jane Steinsnyder, *Long Vest*, 2001; ethnic textiles (cotton and raffia cloth) on black linen, African beads, hand embroidery.
Photo: John Carlano

ANNA CARLSON

ST. PAUL, MINNESOTA

"SINCE 1986, I HAVE BEEN COMBINING
MANY DIFFERENT ELEMENTS INTO RICH
AND VARIED LANDSCAPES. MY WORK IS
COLOR, PATTERN, AND TEXTURE—CREATING
A SPACE FOR EXPERIENCES TO HAPPEN."

The working method of fiber
artist Anna Carlson might be compared to that of a
sculptor. Her thoughts about each piece begin and end
with the whole as she envisions the garment in its final
three-dimensional form on the body. The years that she
has spent altering and combining fabrics through dyeing,
texturing, and sewing afford her the freedom to skillfully
and intuitively build her garments.

Her work is a conscious act of tranforming the mundane
into the interesting. In her artist's statement, she tries to
translate into words the process that engages her in the
studio:

> Rich and varied surfaces fascinate me. Layering
> color, piecing, appliqué, and stitching are techniques
> I use to create surfaces that become invitations to
> come closer, explore the texture and pattern,

Opposite page:
**Anna Carlson, *Louisa's Coat*, 1998; velveteen;
hand dyed, stitched, appliquéd.
Collection of Louisa Williams.**
Photo: Warwick Green

Right:
**Anna Carlson, *Celestial Evening*, 1998; velveteen;
hand dyed, stitched, appliquéd, beaded.**
Photo: Warwick Green

become surrounded by the richness. Piecing materials that have been dyed and overdyed to a rich suedelike appearance creates the foundation for appliqué and stitching in dancing geometric or elegant organic patterns.

In her childhood, she drew sketches of gowns and garments for imaginary characters. Later, her inclinations led her to seek and earn a degree in fashion design from the University of Minnesota, followed by a semester of study at Parsons School of Design in New York. The time at Parsons clarified that she wanted to move in a less industry-driven direction, and she embraced the challenge of making art-to-wear. She learned more about surface design through workshops and individual study and has been creating wearable work since 1986.

Several years ago, she developed a method of texturing fabrics that has become a signature technique. First, she hand-dyes all of the fabrics with a shibori technique. Fabric that has been dyed and washed many times (and therefore preshrunk) is stitched to a backing fabric and embellished with stitching and appliqué in a free-form fashion. Often she adds painted areas to the fabric. This stitched fabric montage is washed again to create a distressed appearance. To create contrast, she sometimes juxtaposes this textured with untextured fabric. Her working method involves both planning and improvisation, as she responds to relationships between shapes and colors used to compose her work.

She sums up her personal connection to her work with the following statement:

With an artist's sensibility, I design and create coats and jackets that combine beautiful colors, rich surfaces, and excellent contruction. I sign each piece by hand as I would a letter to a friend: "Here is what I think; read, interpret, and enjoy."

Above:
Anna Carlson, *Brown Shawl Collar Jacket*, 1998; corduroy and velveteen; hand dyed, appliquéd, stitched.
Photo: Warwick Green

Opposite page:
Anna Carlson, *Klimt Coat*, 1996; corduroy and velveteen; hand dyed, pieced, stitched, appliquéd. Collection of Rosanne Nathanson.
Photo: Wayne Torborg

HULDA
BRIDGEMAN
SPOKANE, WASHINGTON

"MY WORK BEGINS WITH CHOOSING COLORS. I USE COLOR INTUITIVELY, HOLDING FABRICS TOGETHER TO SEE WHICH COMBINATIONS EXCITE MY EYE. I ALSO LIKE THE COMPLEXITY RESULTING FROM 'CONTROLLED' ACCIDENTAL EFFECTS IN BOTH DYEING AND, LATER, PIECING THE FABRICS. TUCKING IS LAID OVER THE PIECING TO BLEND AREAS AND CREATE A RELIEF SURFACE WITH AN ORGANIC, OFTEN RIPPLING TEXTURE, AND A SENSE OF MOVEMENT. ALONG WITH COLOR, MY WORK USUALLY INVOLVES THE JUXTAPOSITION OF TEXTURES WHICH PLAY AGAINST ONE ANOTHER."

Above:
Hulda Bridgeman, *Coat*, 1995; silks; hand dyed, pieced, tucked, stitched.
Photo: Jim Osen. Model: Leslie Laursen

Below:
Hulda Bridgeman, *Jacket*, 1996; silks; hand dyed, pieced, tucked, stitched.
Photo: Jim Osen. Model: Leslie Laursen

Opposite page:
Hulda Bridgeman, *Coat*, 1997; silks; hand dyed, pieced, tucked, stitched.
Photo: Jim Osen. Model: Leslie Laursen

Hulda Bridgeman's life has taken her from the gentle, settled mountains of Virginia to the rugged, evolving landscape of Washington State. She acknowledges the influence of the landscape in her work and approaches surface design with the eye of a painter.

Today her work reflects the coloration and shifting rhythm of the Western landscape. She notes the similarity between the interrupted, unpredictable fractures made in the earth at fault lines and the angled juxtapositions of shapes in her work.

She began her foray into fiber arts many years ago when she taught herself how to weave in order to pass this craft on to her junior high school students. She worked for 16 years as a weaver and dyer before she began building garments by piecing and tucking fabrics. Today, she works in tandem with her husband, Ken, a former attorney who now helps her with everything from ironing to engineering the drape of the cloth.

She still relishes the dye process that she uses on her silks, and the unexpected variations that add depth and interest. After dyeing, she pieces the silks together in a process-oriented way. Then she sews varying and sometimes irregular tucks in the fabric, which further alter the surface and create a sculptural effect. All of the tucks are sewn in black thread, regardless of the color of the fabric. She thinks of these tucks and their underlying colored silks as pen and ink lines on top of color washes. These linear rhythms dominate the shapes that further define her compelling work.

Left:
Hulda Bridgeman, *Coat*, 1993; silks; hand dyed; hand-printed cottons (accents); pieced, stitched.
Photo: Jim Osen. Model: Leslie Laursen

Opposite page, left:
Hulda Bridgeman, *Jacket*, 2001; silks; hand dyed; pieced, tucked; stitched.
Photo: J. Craig Sweat. Model: Leslie Laursen

Opposite page, right:
Hulda Bridgeman, *Jacket*, 2000; silks; hand dyed, pieced, tucked, stitched; fin inserts.
Photo: Jim Osen. Model: Amy Brandon

JANE DUNNEWOLD

SAN ANTONIO, TEXAS

"MY GOAL IS TO CREATE A CLOTH SURFACE THAT HAS VISUAL INTEGRITY—IT IS BALANCED, THERE IS CONTRAST, AND THE SURFACE COULD RIVAL ANY PAINTING IN TERMS OF COLOR AND DESIGN DEVELOPMENT. ADD TO THAT THE IMPORTANCE OF MAINTAINING THE 'HAND' OF THE CLOTH, AND MY FIRST GOAL IS MET. MY SECOND GOAL IS TO MAKE A CLOTH SURFACE THAT IS MORE THAN JUST A PRETTY PIECE OF CLOTH. I WANT TO REFLECT ON THE SURFACE AS I WORK, AND ON THE RELATIONSHIPS I AM DEVELOPING. I LIKE THE IDEA OF TELLING A STORY, OF MAKING THE SURFACE A FORM OF VISUAL POETRY. THIS APPROACH ALLOWS ME TO THINK OF THE CLOTH AS AN OBJECT WHICH IS COMPLETE IN AND OF ITSELF. IF IT GOES ON TO BECOME PART OF A GARMENT, THEN IT'S VISUALLY POETIC ASPECT CONTRIBUTES TO THE GARMENT'S STORY AND APPEAL."

Jane Dunnewold's theory is that "...we all have to make a lot of junk in order to realize our few masterpieces." Since 1995, Dunnewold has focused her artistic energies on the making of what she calls "complex cloth"——the results of the addition and subtraction of layers of dye and painting to yield a surface filled with depth and visual interest. A passionate trial-and-error approach to this subject has brought her recognition as a surface designer, teacher, and author.

Finding her true calling took many years. One of her fondest childhood memories is the experience of watching a group of women quilt at her father's church in Ohio. In college she studied psychology and religion, but spent her spare time sewing and embroidering. When she was 20, she moved to Boston to attend a seminar course in quilting at the Massachusetts College of Art, pursuing her growing interest in fiber arts. About a year later, she moved to San Antonio, Texas, where she

Opposite page:

Jane Dunnewold, Untitled cloth (detail), 2001; silk broadcloth; dyed, overdyed, discharged, screen printed multiple times, foiled.

Photo: Jane Dunnewold

Above:

Jane Dunnewold, Untitled cloth (detail), 2000; silk crepe; dyed, discharged, screen printed multiple times, foiled.

Photo: Jane Dunnewold

As a teacher it is very clear that the 'pack' is behind you and wants to duplicate what you are doing—partially to know how to do it, partially out of admiration for the teacher's work, and partially because human beings are copiers at heart. Accepting this rather than fighting it gives me the urge to keep moving and playing, and keeps me out of ruts.

In 1983, Dunnewold began collaborating with fiber artist Renita Kuhn, who create garments from her cloth. Kuhn became interested in fiber while living in the Bay Area of California in the early 1980s. After leaving a corporate job, she began to design professionally in 1982. Using the creations of local textile artists, she created ethnically-oriented clothing that combined artist-made cloth and textiles from other cultures. Kuhn's interest in a variety of cultural influences stemming from India, Africa, and the Orient are compatible with Dunnewold's aesthetics. Together, they seek to create works that are timeless and universal. Her collaboration with Dunnewold has been ongoing, and, as she describes it, devoid of jealousy or competition. When speaking of the strength of their collaboration, Kuhn notes that she is impressed with Dunnewold's "open-mindedness, dedication, and devotion to her art, as well as her generosity and willingness to share."

ended up taking classes at the Southwest Craft Center in subjects such as embroidery and appliqué.

Years later, she persuaded the director of the Southwest Craft Center to hire her to begin a surface design program to teach students techniques such as silk-screen printing, dyeing, stamping, and stencilling. She began the program with three classes. When she left in 2001, the program boasted 20 classes. Now on her own as a teacher, Dunnewold holds several workshops a year that are always filled. She is an inspiring mentor for her students, and speaks frankly about her willingness to pass on information:

Opposite page, left:

Jane Dunnewold, Untitled, 1998; silk and rayon; pieced, dyed, screen printed, foiled; fabric appliqués of ultra suede; beaded embellishment. Construction and embellishment by Renita Kuhn.

Photo: Jane Dunnewold

Model: Zenna James

Opposite page, right:

Jane Dunnewold, Untitled cloth (detail), 2001; silk broadcloth; dyed, overdyed, discharged, screen printed multiple times, foiled.

Photo: Jane Dunnewold

Left:

Jane Dunnewold, *Kimono*, 1996; cotton; dyed, screen-printed multiple times, foiled. Construction and embellishment by Renita Kuhn.

Photo: Jane Dunnewold

Model: Kim Corbin

TIM
HARDING
STILLWATER, MINNESOTA

"IN PAINTING THE PICTURE PLANE IS THE WINDOW THROUGH WHICH THE
AUDIENCE MUST LOOK TO EXPERIENCE THE ARTIST'S VISION. THAT PLANE IS
ALSO PERHAPS THE ULTIMATE BARRIER BETWEEN ART AND LIFE. CAN THE ARTIST
EVER BREAK THAT BARRIER AND INVOLVE THE VIEWER IN THE CREATIVE ACT:
CAN THE VIEWER EVER BE 'IN' THE WORK?"

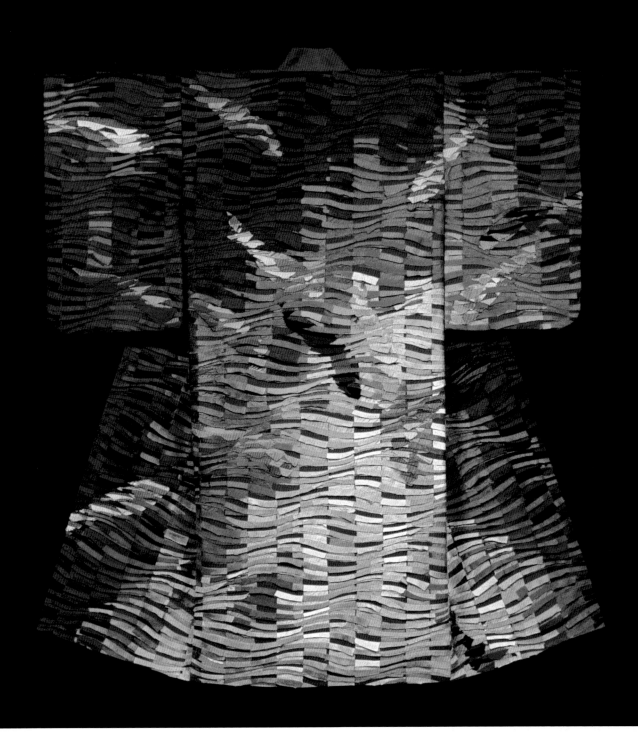

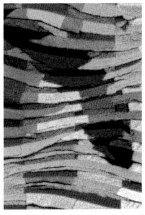

Opposite page:
**Tim Harding, *Aspen*, 1987;
cotton; dyed, layered,
quilted, slashed, frayed.**
Photo: Petronella Ytsma

Above:
**Tim Harding, *Koi Kimono*, 1996;
silk; layered, stitched, cut, pressed.**
Photo: Petronella Ytsma

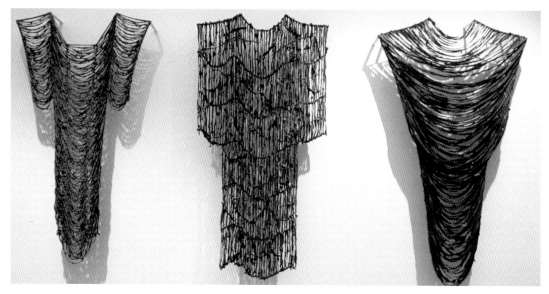

With the eye of a surgeon who knows the anatomy of the world beneath his scalpel, Tim Harding cuts through layers of fabric in a revealing way. The armature of clothing, on which he hangs his formal considerations, is secondary to his obsession with texture, color, line, and mark.

Harding began his artistic life as a painter, often applying layers of paint to his canvas before scratching the surface to disclose some of the painting's underbelly. He found the canvas of his paintings more interesting than the paint. Intrigued by the textural possibilities of the medium of fabric, he returned to school to study art at the Minneapolis College of Art and Design in Minnesota.

In 1979, he developed a technique for building up a "complex structure" of fabric by dyeing, layering, and quilting before "revealing color, image, and pattern

through the mutilation of its surface" by slashing and fraying. This technique—although it has been used to serve a progression of concepts—has remained a constant in his work for more than 20 years.

In 1986, he began layering and slashing heavy cottons sewn into the forms of greatcoats and kimonos. During the later part of the 1980s, he did a series of landscapes on coats with references to nature. Using the fabric as a painter would use paint, he slashed and pressed the fabric to create patterns that suggested trees, clouds, or water. By the 1990s, he found that he favored the intense colors and vulnerable surface of silk over cotton, and his work became more and more an abstraction of nature than a nod at representing it.

In his present work, he creates not only clothing but wall pieces that allow him to explore the visual properties of color and texture without the added consideration of the garment's shape. Whether his work takes the form of wall pieces or garments, it constantly challenges assumptions about art and craft by not bending to categorization.

In a more recent series of work, he has turned to the study of the properties of light on water, dealing with reflection and refraction. Although he still uses nature as a point of departure, it almost seems unnecessary. Harding is by nature a colorist who explores the endless formal and emotive possibilities of his subject matter.

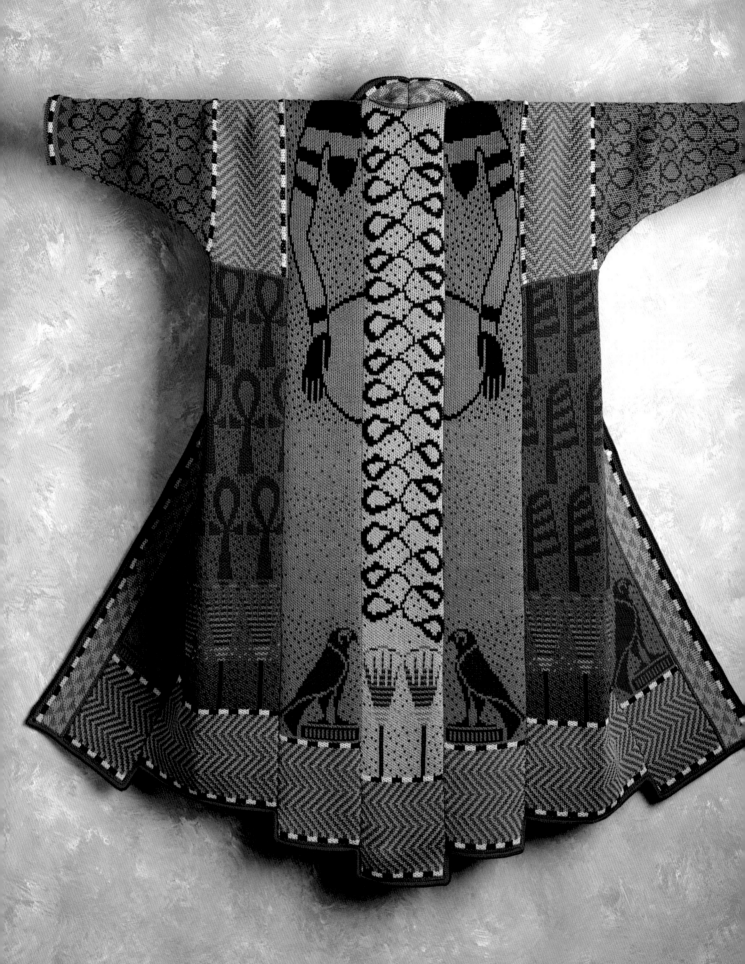

SUSAN SUMMA

SANTE FE, NEW MEXICO

"I INHERITED A SENSE OF LONGING FOR THE FOREIGN, THE UNKNOWN, THE UNCHARTED—A SENSE OF EXOTIC COLOR AND PATTERN, AND A COMPULSION TO EXPLORE A CULTURE NOT MY OWN....OF ALL MY CHILDHOOD MEMORIES THAT I HOLD DEAR, THE BEST OF THEM IS OF THE EXOTIC COLORS, PATTERNS, AND TEXTURES OF THE SILK GARMENTS MY GREAT-AUNT SUE BROUGHT BACK FROM CHINA FOR ME AND MY SISTER MYRA, FOR CHRISTMAS OF 1950.... I AM DESCENDED FROM AN ADVENTURESS, ONE WHO TRAVELED FAR AND WIDE AND CAME BACK WITH EXOTIC FABRICS, STORIES AND SONGS IN A LANGUAGE WE DIDN'T UNDERSTAND, WHO CREATED A SENSE OF ADVENTURE THAT HAS INFLUENCED MY WORLD."

When Susan Summa discovered her innate love for textiles at age two, and later studied interior design in college, she couldn't know what life would bring her. After graduating from the University of Texas at Austin, she worked as an interior designer in Dallas and Austin. During this period, a client encouraged her to study weaving, and she found that she was "passionate about the feel of yarn, the multitude of colors...and the meditative process" involved in making cloth.

She left Texas to move to Sante Fe in the late 1970s. Since there was little or no interior design work for her in her new location, she decided to weave tapestries on her loom and made a business of it for awhile. But the work was extremely tedious and took too long to satisfy

Opposite page:
Susan Summa, *Tears of the Goddess*, 1998; cotton and rayon; loom knitted, crochet detail.
Photo: Doug Merriam. Courtesy of Santa Fe Weaving Gallery; Sante Fe, New Mexico

Above:
Susan Summa, *Andean Homage Caravelli Coat*, c.1996; cotton; loom knitted, crochet detail.
Photo: Valerie Santagto. Courtesy of Santa Fe Weaving Gallery; Sante Fe, New Mexico

her many ideas for color and design. When she discovered that something called a "knitting machine" (or "knitting loom" as it was called in Europe) existed, she realized that it not only fit her existing skills as a weaver, but could produce cloth much faster. The knitted panels that she made were not suited in structure for hanging on the wall, so she turned to making clothing.

She was in the right place at the right time, as the saying goes. The American Craft Movement was gaining momentum, and art-to-wear was coming into its own in the craft field—which allowed her the possibility of making a living creating wearable art. She remembers those earlier days: "When I started, there were only a handful of artwear designers/makers, and most of us were doing outrageous, experimental garments with great energy in the design content, and less in the actual fit of the body!"

She founded a small business called Summa Design and made a living creating limited production and one-of-a-kind garments. Always driven by the possibilities of color and pattern (that she saves in bits and pieces in a loose file), her themes have ranged from ancient universal motifs to a current interest in abstract surface design. When those who are aware of her love of color and design ask why she doesn't "just paint them on fabric," she notes a "deep satisfaction from handling the textures of the yarns."

Over the past few years, she has produced for the high-end marketplace, designing several collections a year (one inspired by her early introduction to Chinese clothing), and leaving behind the production end of making artwear as much as possible. She reflects on the fact that "the more I moved into being a business savvy artwear producer, with employees, the more I felt I was moving away from the truly creative aspects of my work." Like so many artists, she has struggled to balance the need to make a living with a desire to make pieces that reflect new ideas.

Perhaps this recognition of the often dichotomous nature of business and art prepared her to serve in an entrepreneurial role not only for herself but for others. Seven years ago, she went to New York during market week to look for a venue beyond the craft shows that she'd been doing for many years. She didn't find a show that seemed right, so she eventually founded a group of artwear designers known as Atelier. The group's show has been a huge success and is now held three times a year to show "exclusive collections of womenswear and accessories to the wholesale trade" during the weeks when buyers (normally seeking ready-to-wear garments) come to New York from all over the world. By breaking into this market, Atelier has brought exposure and business to many artists at a different level.

Summa hopes to balance making special work with her vision of continuing to advance the field of art-to-wear. She finds her most recent role as advocate very satisfying and shares her perspective on a movement that is now more than three decades old:

> The beginnings of art-to-wear are rooted in simply making something which can (sort of) fit a body, but the art is the most important part of the equation. Unfortunately, most of the public still percieves art- to-wear in this way: something funky, sometimes gaudy, which doesn't fit very well, and has limited places you can wear it. But art- to-wear has grown up during the last 10 years. There are now many very sophisticated garments being made, with exquisite texture and fit, which have formed a new category, which I call "artisanal couture."

Perhaps "wearable art/art-to-wear/artwear/artisanal couture" will continue to evolve, along with its name, through the dedication of Summa and many others.

Opposite page:
Susan Summa, *Double Happiness*, 2000; cotton; rayon, wool; loom knitted, crochet detail.
Photo: Doug Merriam. Courtesy of Santa Fe Weaving Gallery; Sante Fe, New Mexico

Right:
Susan Summa, *Chambers of the Heart*, 1997; cotton, loom knitted with hand crocheted embellishment.
Photo: Valerie Santagto. Courtesy of Santa Fe Weaving Gallery; Sante Fe, New Mexico

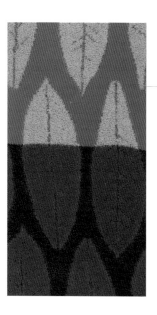

ANN CLARKE
SYRACUSE, NEW YORK

"MY DESIGN PROCESS IS LIKE LIVING BY A RIVER FED BY SPRINGS AND UNKNOWN SOURCES FAR AWAY. THERE ARE CONSTANTS, THERE ARE CYCLICAL VARIATIONS, THERE ARE TIMES WHEN UNEXPECTED THINGS FLOAT BY. THERE ARE THINGS TOSSED IN BY OTHER PEOPLE, AND THERE ARE WAYS I MAY ALTER THE FLOW. THE CONSTANTS IN MY WORK ARE TELLING A STORY WITH IMAGE AND COLOR IN THE FORM OF HEAVY WOOL COATS. THE THEMES I CYCLE THROUGH ARE FAMILY HISTORY, NATURE, LITERARY REFERENCES (POETRY AND FICTION), AND STORIES FROM WORLD NEWS. I BEGIN WITH THE STORY."

The narrative of Ann Clarke's work is woven from small bits and pieces of information that she synergizes into a fascinating whole. Her coats of many colors evolve from a lifetime of experiences and observations.

Several years ago, she hiked to a waterfall on a winter camping trip and discovered the inspiration for one of her pieces in the waters at the base of the fall where a small frozen dragonfly sparkling with color tossed like a tiny jewel in the cold waters. She was able to retrieve the creature and replicate its tender textures through a photographic scanner. From a host of sources such as this, her work incorporates what she calls a "lexicon of images and patterns" that she uses as a kind of "pictographic vocabulary." Tree limbs, leaves, faces, hands, and textured patterns are all potential subject matter for her work.

From conception to completion, she works like a collage artist, gathering images, juxtaposing and arranging them

into compositions, repeating them, and sometimes altering them. Embracing chance occurrences, she describes the arranging of images that will later be transposed to fabric: "As I shuffle the pieces, I begin to recognize a visual system in the disorder that I am interested in." Later, after the fabric is knitted and fulled, she pins together and arranges the pieces until they feel right, often making unplanned decisions. Fully engaged by the process of the work until the end, she adds touches of needlepoint or embroidery to the assembled garment where they seem appropriate, overlaying rich textures with more tactile and visual interest.

In 1981, she completed a degree in printmaking and painting from the University of Michigan at Ann Arbor and moved to Chicago, Illinois, to begin her life as an artist. Living in a small space where she could no longer create large pieces, she decided to "shrink" her work. She began incorporating handwork techniques that she had learned from her mother, using stitching on paintings, for instance.

As this work evolved, her twin sister—who was a law student at the time—took up knitting. Clarke was fascinated with the process and couldn't resist giving her sister suggestions about color and design. After enough interference, her sister firmly took her by the hand in order to teach her how to knit her own sweaters. She started to make unusual sweaters, and received so many encouraging comments that she contacted galleries and began to sell her wearable work in the late 1980s.

After several years of making each piece by hand, she developed debilitating carpal tunnel syndrome. Forced to look at other options, she embraced the "intermediate technology" of the knitting machine—a decision that provided her with the means to develop much more complex work with a high level of image definition on a small scale within the fabric's structure.

Opposite page left:
Ann Clarke, *Into the Woods*, 2000; machine knit, felted wool, needlepoint.
Photo: Dave Revette. Model: Jacqueline Jager-Muench

Center:
Ann Clarke, *Quilted Jacket of Monks*, 2000; machine knit, felted wool, needlepoint, embroidery and other handstitching; pearls, garnets.
Photo: Dave Revette. Model: Jacqueline Jager-Muench

Above:
Ann Clarke, *Mimicry*, 2001; machine knit, felted wool, silk, cotton, running stitches.
Photo: Dave Revette. Model: Jacqueline Jager-Muench

Her present technique involves many steps beginning with concepts for surface design taken from photocopies made from collected photos, drawings, or actual objects. She spreads the copies on the floor before arranging, cutting, and pasting them to make compilation images. (She compares this process to reading tea leaves because it is intuitive and improvisational.) This pattern is then photocopied and put into repeat before being transferred with graphite pencils to polyester film sheets. It is then read by the knitting machine, and a "memory card" is produced that is about the size of a charge card. Using any number of these cards with stored information, she can arrange the images in any sequence, and the machine will set up the knitting needles on the machine bed to knit the rows. Among other options, she is able to repeat the pattern, expand it, or mirror it. Each row that is done by the machine requires handwork to tack down stitches and maintain the integrity of the fabric. The knitting is very loosely done to allow for shrinking (fulling) later.

After completion, the knitted panels are washed six or more times followed by brushing in between until the fabric integrates into a felted whole. Using her own patterns, she cuts out the pieces from various panels, arranging them as she goes. The seams are sewn with a sewing machine followed by the hand stitching and embroidery.

She loves the whole process because it "carries her love of image and color over into fiber work." She has found a breadth through her medium that she might not have found had she chosen something else: "Fiber allows me to add 'the hand' or the feel and the juxtaposition of textures and function to the 'palette.'"

Opposite page:
Ann Clarke, *Laurel Blanket*, 1998; machine knit, felted wool, needlepoint, crochet. Collection of Errol Willet and Jen Gandee.
Photo: Peter Montonti

Left:
Ann Clarke, *Northern Lights Coat*, 1991; handknit wool, cotton, needlepoint.
Photo: Gary Lee Heard

Right:

Robin L. Bergman, *How To Mend a Broken Heart: Chenille Duster Coat and Evening Bag* **1993; raw silk, rayon, rayon chenille, lurex; loom knit.**

Photo: Gordon S. Bernstein

Model: Bevoir Brown

Opposite page, top left:

Robin L. Bergman, *Bronze/Cinnamon Chenille Maple Jacket and Scarf,* 2000; raw silk, rayon, rayon chenille; loom knit.

Photo: Gordon S. Bernstein

Model: Karima El-Baz

Opposite page, top right:

Robin L. Bergman, *Chenille Circles Y Peplum Vest, Scarf, Gloves, and Square Hat,* 2001; raw silk, rayon, rayon chenille; loom knit.

Photo: Gordon S. Bernstein

Model Karima: El-Baz

ROBIN L.
BERGMAN
CONCORD, MASSACHUSETTS

"LOOM KNITTING IS A MANUAL PROCESS LIKE WEAVING
USING A KNITTING MACHINE. THE MAKING OF KNITTED
WORK IS PARTICULARLY CHALLENGING BECAUSE THE FABRIC,
PATTERNING, AND SHAPED GARMENT PIECES ARE CREATED
SIMULTANEOUSLY....MY EMPHASIS IS ON TREATING THE
SURFACE LIKE A CANVAS, EXPERIMENTING WITH SURFACE
DESIGN AND UNUSUAL JUXTAPOSITIONS OF COLOR, TEXTURE,
AND PATTERN—IN EFFECT, PAINTING WITH YARNS."

Right:

Robin L. Bergman,
Peluche Shawl and
Eyelash Mesh Dress,
2001; viscose, rayon,
rayon chenille, vintage
beads; loom knit.
Photo: Gordon S. Bernstein
Model: Karima El-Baz

Below, right:
Robin L. Bergman, *Thyme*
Long Tapestry Coat,
Scarf, and Square Hat
and Beaded Vines Cuff
Bracelet, **1999; raw silk,**
rayon, rayon chenille;
loom knit (coat, scarf,
hat); Japanese delica
glass seed beads, Czech
glass beads; square stitch
off-loom technique
(bracelet).
Photo: Gordon S. Bernstein
Model: Venera Tabaku

Opposite page:
Robin L. Bergman, *Aishes*
Chayil: Sabbath
Ceremonial Coat, **1998;**
raw silk, rayon, rayon
chenille; loom knit.
Commissioned for the
Jewish Women's Archives
of Boston Oral History
Project. In memory of
Fannie Zimmerman
Goldberg (1907-1997).
Collection of Fran and
Don Putnoi.
Photo: Gordon S. Bernstein

While Robin Bergman was
working toward a graduate degree in painting at the
Maryland Institute College of Art in Baltimore, she
painted during the day to fulfill her studio requirements,
while sewing and knitting at night. Luckily, she studied
under painter Grace Hartigan, who was enlightened to
the fact that all media are created equal—whether
paints, yarns, or fabrics. Hartigan encouraged her to
bring her passion for fiber into the studio, and Bergman
combined paint and fabric.

After graduating with an M.F.A. in 1980, she worked as a
textile conservator in Boston and knitted during her time
off. Several years later, she felt a pull to return to her art-

work. When she discovered knitting machines in a store,
a light went off, and she knew that working on a larger
scale was something that might work for her. Propelled by
her belief that she could make a living doing work that
she loved, she rented a studio and undertook the tedious
work of learning to use a less-than-perfect knitting
machine. Several months later, despite the skepticism of
those around her, she quit her job.

Her early, passionate inclination has taken her far in her
field. A few years ago, she began using a computer as a
tool to enhance her process. The computer is hooked to
the knitting machine, and, in turn, the knitting machine
reads the specifications that Bergman inputs. Although
this technology has greatly increased her ability to produce and given her more time to design, the process is
far from simple. As she explains, every knitted piece
must be conceived and made at once because the stitch
structure of the knit determines the design. She now

has a small staff that includes knitters and part-time stitchers to assist her with the process, but she must shape and size each garment individually, check the tension of the yarn, and watch for breaks in the pattern or color. Because most garments use 20 to 30 yarn colors, and yarns have different gauges, the orchestration of a piece demands skill derived from years of experience.

She uses richly colored yarns made of a variety of fibers including rayon, rayon chenille, raw silk, cotton, wool, and cashmere to make jackets, coats, tunics, shawls, scarves, hats, and gloves. Her textured surfaces are punctuated with calligraphic designs that lead the eye

from one area of stimulation to another. She is known ·for juxtaposing colors and patterning with an expression-istic exuberance tamed by an innate ability to effectively compose the whole. She synthesizes a host of influ-ences including African and Japanese patterns, antique rugs and weavings, woodblock prints, Elizabethan, and Medieval designs. Appropriately compared to tapestries, her work is an ongoing exploration of relationships between color, design, and materials.

LORIE JOHNSON

**TOKYO, JAPAN &
WELLESLEY FARMS,
MASSACHUSETTS**

"FELTING IS THE CLOSEST MEDIUM I HAVE FOUND THAT MIRRORS MY DESIRE OF EXPRESSION IN TEXTILES....I LIKE TO THINK ABOUT MY WORK AS OBJECTS OR SCULPTURES, RATHER THAN AS ACCESSORIES, JACKETS, OR CARPETS. BUT, PERSONALLY, I WISH THE WORK TO BE PRACTICAL ENOUGH TO BE USED....I WANT EACH PIECE TO DEMON-STRATE THE ULTIMATE CAPABILITIES OF WOOL DURING ITS SHRINKING PROCESS, EITHER BY ITSELF OR WITH OTHER MATERIALS AND TECHNI-CAL EFFECTS ON THE WOOL, SUCH AS COLOR AND FIBER BLENDING, AFTER-DYEING, OR BURNING....IT IS ALWAYS A SURPRISE TO ME WHEN FIRST-TIME CLIENTS DON'T RECOGNIZE THE MATERIAL AS WOOL IN THE PRODUCTS BECAUSE THE EFFECT IS SO UNLIKE ANYTHING THEY'VE SEEN BEFORE."

Above:
Jorie Johnson, *Seamless*, 2001; exhibition installation at Wacoal Art Space Ginza, Tokyo, Japan; hand-felted seamless garments and hand-felted assembled mufflers; shibori-dyed shawls with needle-felted embellishment.

Photo: M. Suemasa

Right:
Jorie Johnson, *Confetti (from Shawl Body Wrap Series)*, 2001; wool, printed silk organza, novelty yarns, peacock feathers; machine and hand felted.

Photo: T. Ito

Above:

Jorie Johnson, *Autumn Breezes*, 2000; knit mohair (sleeves), wool, printed silk organza, copper fabric, novelty yarns; hand felted, machine-stitched embellishment.

Photo: Y. Okumoto

Below:

Jorie Johnson, *Be My Valentine*, 2000; knit mohair (sleeves), wool, printed silk organza, novelty yarns, knitted fabric, buttons, beads; hand felted, machine-stitched embellishment.

Photo: Y. Okumoto

Jorie Johnson is an American citizen who moved her studio and business to Tokyo over 12 years ago out of an instinctive desire to be in the milieu of artists who have historically considered textiles as a serious art form. "I am somewhat of a nomad at heart," notes Johnson, who studied textiles at the Helsinki University of Art and Design in Finland as well as at Rhode Island School of Design in the United States. Her work as an artist, designer and owner of Joe Rae Textiles, teacher, and author moves her to and fro around the globe—promoting her work, doing research and writing, and teaching workshops.

She has taken one of what she calls the "oldest of manipulated fiber techniques" and the "oldest body covering produced by man" to create extremely contemporary, cutting-edge works in the field of fiber. She builds and shapes pieces that embrace as well as defy their origin in ancient, traditional feltmaking techniques. "The enhancement of the appreciation [of feltmaking] as a visual art form, and its integration into the modern world of fashion fabrics is my ambition," says Johnson.

To create her practical art, she manipulates single wool fibers through a series of complex processes that include the layering of fibers that are dampened, pounded, and massaged before they meld and shrink together to form an integrated whole. Through long years of experimentation with timing and touch, she works with the instinct of a sculptor who shapes and molds the final piece in an intuitive fashion. No needles or thread bind the edges of her seams, but rather the natural results of the shrunken fibers. As she explains about the process:

> I start by layering the wool while designing the outer design motifs and shape...one has to learn how to control the loose fibers into a perfect quality and weight fabric by coaxing [them] to run the course you have chosen for them....Touch and feel and sense are important to feltmaking. We are not working with warp and weft threads stretched on a loom, nor knitting loops into a structure, but

controlling wool fibers which by themselves are nothing but fluffy piles of protein filaments. There is no strength to them individually until they enter the shrinking process, and as they mass together, the strength potential is revealed.

She begins with naturally colored and dyed wool that has been carded so that the fibers are aligned and easy to control when building up layers for both two-dimensional and three-dimensional pieces. She is extremely selective about the wools that she uses, down to researching which ones provide the best possible effects in terms of shrinkage and other considerations.

The touch of her hand is always evident in the final pieces whose surfaces have a depth that results from the long process of integrating fibers to create designs. In essence, Johnson draws and paints her surfaces with dyed woolen fibers. This creative part of the process interests her the most, and she focuses as much time as possible on composing with her medium. Never interested in making something "simply because it might sell," Johnson earnestly pursues her art with the love and dedication of one who wishes to contribute something to the world that embodies enduring and hopeful resonance.

Above:
Jorie Johnson, *Stained Glass: Rusted from Muffler Series*, 2000; felted wool, Indian cotton; hand felted.
Photo: M. Suemasa

Left:
Jorie Johnson, *Stained Glass: Rusted from Muffler Series* (detail), 2000; felted wool, Indian cotton; hand felted.
Photo: M. Suemasa

JEAN WILLIAMS CACICEDO
BERKELEY, CALIFORNIA

"CLOTH HAS THE ABILITY TO TRANSFORM
IDEAS AND THE POWER TO SEDUCE THE EYE
AND HAND. I LOVE MY MATERIALS AND MY
PROCESS...AS TEDIOUS AS IT MAY BE AT TIMES.
I LOVE EVERYTHING ABOUT TEXTILES, AND I
LOVE THE FACT THAT YOU CAN WEAR A COAT,
BUT YOU CAN'T WEAR A PAINTING."

When Jean Williams Cacicedo
was a child, she carefully arranged dollhouse furniture in shoe boxes, building small architectural kingdoms from her imagination. At an early age, she was interested in the structure of things, and that interest has compelled her to stretch the boundaries of the definitions of both art and craft.

During 2000, Cacicedo was honored with a 30-year retrospective of her work, exhibited at the Museum of Craft and Folk Art in San Francisco, California. Curated by Carole Austin, the show documented the wide range of Cacicedo's artistic inquisitiveness: from her early knitted and crocheted work created in the 1970s, when wearable art emerged as an alternative to main-stream art, to her more recent exploration of surface design through slashing and shibori.

Cacicedo studied sculpture and painting at Pratt Institute in Brooklyn, where she made freestanding sculptures that eventually evolved into work that she thought of as sculptures for the body. Crochet and knitting combined with materials such as leather, wool, and fur composed her first garments, which now seem to embody the spirit of the early days of art-to-wear. During this period, she met Julie Schafler Dale, founder and owner of Julie's Artisans Gallery in New York, who encouraged her and sold her work. It was through this gallery that she found her first market and audience, and she still shows at the gallery today.

By the 1980s, she was making pieced and dyed coats and vests from shrunken (fulled) woven wool, with remnants of crochet and knitting. From studying molas, she adopted reverse appliqué as a means of integrating design elements and garment construction. The visual depth that she is able to achieve with this technique has become her trademark, and she continues to be challenged by this method of piecing her vibrant, dyed wools.

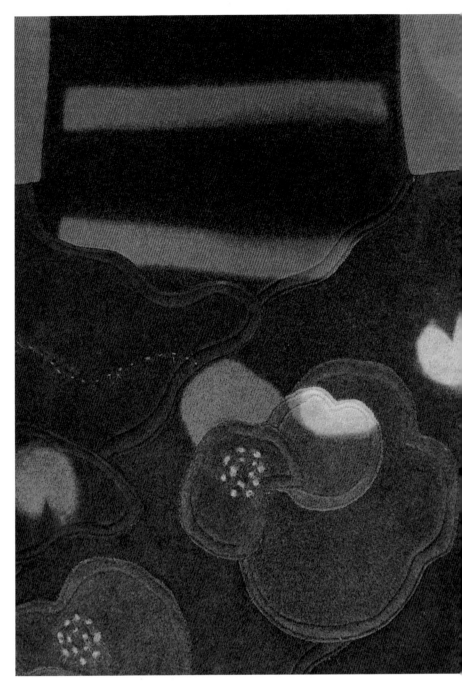

Opposite page, top left:
Jean Williams Cacicedo, *Lotus*, 2000; woven wool and mohair; fulled, clamp resist dyed, knit appliquéd, stitched, shibori.
Photo: Barry Shapiro

Opposite page, bottom left:
Jean Williams Cacicedo, *Aurora Coat*, 2000; wool, clamp resist dyed, fulled, woven.
Photo: Barry Shapiro
Courtesy of Julie Artisan's Gallery; New York

Opposite page, right:
Jean Williams Cacicedo, *Lotus*, 2000; woven wool and mohair; fulled, clamp resist dyed, knit appliquéd, stitched, shibori.
Photo: Barry Shapiro. Model: Anna Schonberg

Above:
Jean Williams Cacicedo, *Lotus* (detail), 2000; woven wool and mohair; fulled, clamp resist dyed, knit appliquéd, stitched, shibori.
Photo: Barry Shapiro

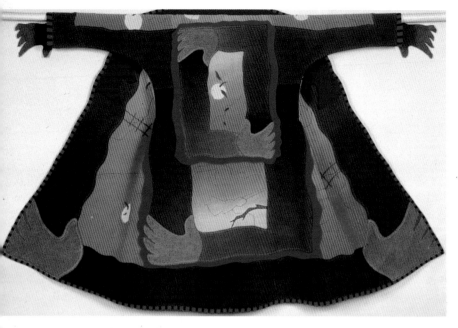

Every piece begins with a drawing on paper in which Cacicedo works out the formal aspects of the largely abstract designs that become her coats and other garments. The final design is then drawn to scale and a paper pattern made. From muslin, she cuts the pieces of the pattern and sews them together to check the fit of the garment. "This pattern is my road map," she explains. "I can piece all I want, and know the final outcome of the construction."

She hand-dyes pieces of her wool that are large enough to create each part of the pattern. Then she refers back to the drawing and begins sewing the parts of her "puzzle" together. The final design emerges as she works. She

Above, top:
Jean Williams Cacicedo, *Coat of Arms*, 1994; woven wool; fulled, dyed, pieced, stitched, appliquéd; knit bands.
Photo: Barry Shapiro. Collection of Bonnie Scott. Courtesy of Santa Fe Weaving Gallery; Sante Fe, New Mexico

Above:
Jean Williams Cacicedo, *About Fate*, 1989; woven wool; fulled, pieced, dyed, reverse appliqué.
Photo: Barry Shapiro

Right:
Jean Williams Cacicedo, *About Fate* (detail), 1989; woven wool; fulled, pieced, dyed, reverse appliqué.
Photo: Barry Shapiro

uses a flat seam construction which cuts down on bulk and allows her to sew seams of any shape she needs to fulfill her design. Because she uses felted wool that doesn't ravel, she can trim close to the stitching on each seam to produce a "clean separation of shapes and colors."

Aside from her technique, which serves her well, Cacicedo's lifework as an artist is deeply spiritual and biographical:

> The work I create comes from my desire to make what I experience both visual and tactile. Process (dyeing, felting and piecing of cloth) and content (ideas, themes that I want to express) form a base to my work, communicating ideas through the visceral language of color and texture. Inspired by personal myths and symbolic imagery, my work tells stories about journeys, both physical and spiritual. Cloth is the basic element to the work.

Her powerful work, so individual and personal, could not have been accomplished without years of contemplation and the ability to make the difficult link between abstract concepts and their material manifestation. She notes influences in her work, but her work is so intrinsically unique that they hardly seem worth mentioning.

The soft, evocative piece titled *Lotus Coat* (2000), made for her retrospective exhibition, is her interpretation of rebirth and her reflection on the turn of the century. Beneath the floating water lilies on the coat's surface seems to lie an infinite depth—perhaps a reflection of the artist's knowledge that there is always more to come.

Right:
Jean Williams Cacicedo, *Rain Coat*, 1998; knit wool; fulled, dyed, slashed, punched.
Photo: Barry Shapiro. Collection of artist. Model: Anna Schonberg

CAROL LEE
SHANKS
BERKELEY, CALIFORNIA

"I STRIVE TO MAKE BEAUTIFULLY SIMPLE, UNSTRUCTURED GARMENTS THAT FEEL GOOD ON THE BODY, FUNCTION WELL, AND ARE EASY TO CARE FOR. INTEGRAL TO THESE IDEALS IS THE ELEMENT OF SURFACE TEXTURE....I LET THE CLOTH LEAD THE WAY. WILL IT DRAPE AGAINST THE BODY EASILY OR DESIRE AN ARCHITECTURAL SHAPE? DOES IT LEND ITSELF TO TEXTURAL MANIPULATION? CAN IT STAND ALONE OR DOES IT REQUIRE OTHER FABRIC PARTNERS?....THE ELEMENTS THAT ARE IMPORTANT TO ME ARE TEXTURE, SHAPE, LAYERING, DETAIL, COLOR, MOTION, AND HOW I CAN COMBINE THEM TO CREATE THE MOST INTERESTING SILHOUETTES. THE TEXTURE MAY ALREADY EXIST WITHIN THE CLOTH, OR I MAY CHOOSE TO ADD TO IT BY MANIPULATION, I.E., WASHING, PLEATING, OR STITCHING."

Right:
Carol Lee Shanks, *Gypsy Series*, 1998; layers of silk velvet and dupioni; hand-spun, dyed, and woven cloth by Kathryn Alexander (top/shirt); design by Shanks.
Photo: Elizabeth Opalenik

Below, left:
Carol Lee Shanks, *Gypsy Series* (detail of sleeve cuffs), 1998; layers of silk velvet and dupioni; handspun, dyed, and woven cloth by Kathryn Alexander (shirt); design by Shanks.
Photo: Elizabeth Opalenik

Below, right:
Carol Lee Shanks, *Fairy Series*, 1998; layers of handpleated and handwoven silks; handspun, dyed, and woven cloth by Kathryn Alexander.
Photo: Elizabeth Opalenik

Carol Lee Shanks' interest in the texture of woven fabric has always served as the point of departure for her work. The seemingly ephemeral layers of her simple but elegant pieces move and respond to the wearer's body, creating a sort of kinetic art full of contrasts among color, pattern, and the underlying structures of the cloth.

Her fascination with cloth grew out of an early interest in sewing. As a teenager she could spend entire days sewing, lost in the process. Later, she went on to earn a degree in Textile and Costume Design from the University of California at Davis before working in the retail clothing business in San Francisco as a buyer's assistant, sales manager, and merchandiser.

Beginning in 1984, she went out on her own, designing clothing from her Berkeley, California, studio. "Making a living and making art feed off of one another for me," she notes, acknowledging that she longs for more time to concentrate on one-of-a-kind pieces instead of limited production pieces. She believes that the demand for limited production work will build her reputation and "validate

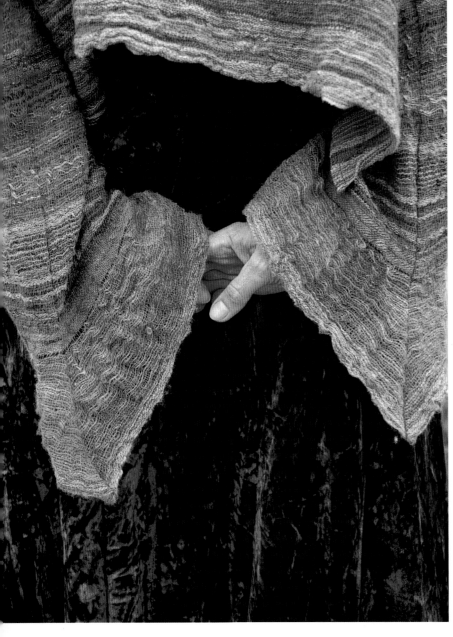

[her] as a prolific and vital working artist." She accepts this challenge as a part of her journey.

She has always found fabrics made by others that interest her and spark her imagination. Today, she works in close collaboration with Kathryn Alexander—a spinner, dyer, and weaver who makes the open-weave, light silks that make up much of her work. The yarns that Alexander uses are singles to which she applies no plying or finishing. Alexander notes that this creates a weave that is "full of energy...springy and lightweight."

The collaboration grew out of each partner eyeing the other's work and admiring it. When Alexander began making a lighter cloth with a lively surface structure, Shanks began envisioning garments to make from it. Today, the designer acknowledges that their collaboration is "one of independent equals in different areas of expertise." This relationship between designer and weaver allows Shanks to concentrate on the area that interests her the most—the creation of visual relationships through layering color, shape, and texture.

Below:
Carol Lee Shanks, *Lillian*, 1999; handspun, dyed, and woven cloth by Kathryn Alexander; design by Shanks.
Photo: Elizabeth Opalenik

RANDALL DARWALL

BASS RIVER, MASSACHUSETTS

"I HAVE ALWAYS LOVED COLOR AND SEEM TO UNDERSTAND IT EMOTIONALLY IN WAYS
THAT I WILL NEVER BE ABLE TO EXPLAIN—BUT FOR WHICH I AM TRULY GRATEFUL. I
PAINTED UNSUCCESSFULLY FOR YEARS BEFORE I DISCOVERED WEAVING AND WAS NEVER
GREAT AT GETTING THE COLOR TO BEHAVE. THE POINTILLIST, OPTICAL BLENDING OF
SMALL SILK THREAD IN THE HIDE AND SEEK OF THE WOVEN STRUCTURES KEEPS THE
COLORS CLEAN BUT ALLOWS FOR EXCITING DYNAMICS TO BEGIN."

Opposite page:

Randall Darwall, *Vest, Jacket, and Scarf,* **1998; silk; hand-dyed yarns, handwoven woven. Design by Brian Murphy.**

Photo: Morgan Rockhill

Above:

Randall Darwall, *Jacket and Shawl,* **1996; silks; woven, hand dyed; twill damask weave jacket combined with sixteen shaft shawl. Design by Brian Murphy.**

Photo: Morgan Rockhill

Left:

Randall Darwall, *Satin Strip Weave Scarf,* **1995; assorted silks; hand dyed, handwoven.**

Photo: Morgan Rockhill

The subject matter of Randall

Darwall's art is color. The warp and the weft of weaving provide him with a stage on which to play out his obsession with this theme. In a statement of purpose that he wrote for his work more than 20 years ago, he stated: "More and more the reason I weave is color: color working through texture, fiber, structure, scale, technique, function." His compelling need for innovation is predicted in the same writing: " I strike out in a direction, but the intuitive urge to vary, to respond to color with more color takes over—and the work evolves. One piece leads to the next; there are too many possibilities in weaving color to ever want to repeat."

Today, he is still exploring a never-ceasing realm of color juxtapositions that he orchestrates into complex patterns. He often compares the combination of colors in his cloth to the notes in jazz—they create resonance and depth when aligned or played off of one another.

And, like a jazz musician, he likes a bit of dissonance, pushing the colors as far as he can while composing with the overall balance of the work in his mind.

His work has also been compared to writing: "His fabric reads with the complexity of a fine novel; it is as intriguing as a road map of a place dreamed of but never visited." (Mary Holden, *The Boston Globe Magazine*, design section, 1986.) In interviews over the years, he stresses the narrative quality of the dialogue that he creates and responds to when engaged in the process of weaving.

Making cloth indulges his highly conceptual, solitary, and intellectual side. The yang that provides balance to this yin is time away from the studio traveling with his partner, Brian Murphy (who designs the clothing that is made from his cloth). Selling work in America and England, teaching workshops, attending conferences, and giving lectures fill the public side of his life. An

added trip to Ireland or other distant shore may provide inspiration for the color and/or structure of new work, or a trip to London may serve the added purpose of finding new yarns.

In a friendly newsletter written by Darwall to patrons of the Smithsonian Craft Show (where he has been a regular for many years), he serves up the details of his life, including the fact that he and Brian have already put 30,000 miles on their new van in one year. He mentions that they need to work on their "website, and all that stuff" when they have the time. He follows this conversational thought with: "Luckily, I've learned that I can't reinvent everything all at once."

Nevertheless, one gets the sense from the accomplishments of his past, and his enthusiastic engagement in the present, that it isn't all that likely that he won't keep trying.

ARLENE WOHL
SAUSALITO, CALIFORNIA

"I MAKE CLOTH FOR THE BODY BECAUSE I LOVE ALL THE TRANSFORMATIONS THAT
HAPPEN ON THE LONG JOURNEY FROM THE SELECTION OF YARNS TO THE COAT ON
THE WEARER'S BACK. I LOVE THE IDEA AND THE PROCESS OF SELECTING DISTINCT
YARNS AND WEAVING THEM INTO A CLOTH SO THAT THE WHOLE IS GREATER THAN
THE SUM OF ITS PARTS, EACH STRAND HAVING LOST A LITTLE OF ITS IDENTITY AS IT
CONTRIBUTES, OFFERS ITSELF TO THE CLOTH..."

Arlene Wohl was first struck

with the desire to be a weaver when she was strolling through
a shopping mall, pregnant, and holding her two-year-old son by the hand.
She noticed a woman demonstrating on a loom and was immediately
entranced. Compelled by a desire to make her own cloth, she took her first
weaving lessons from the woman she met that day.

Opposite page, left:

**Arlene Wohl, *Double-Woven Reversible Jacket*,
2000; cotton gauze and wool; double-faced
structure.**

Photo: Leon Borensztein. Model: Cassandra Trainor

Opposite page, right:

**Arlene Wohl, *Coat in Chevron Weave*, c. 1997; wool,
cotton, rayon, viscose; chevron weave.**

Photo: Barry Brukoff. Model: Claire Salih

Above, left:

**Arlene Wohl, *Long Coat with Contrasting Lapel*,
2001; wool; boulevard weave.**

Photo: Leon Borensztein

Above, right:

**Arlene Wohl, *Coat with Assymetrical Collar*, 2001;
lattice ribbon weft, wool warp; waffle weave.**

Photo: Leon Borensztein

After she gave birth to twins, the weaving became a
"respite from the chaos" of domestic life:

> I became Madame Defarge of weaving, wove into the
> night and dreamed of the next warp even as I dia-
> pered and burped and sang lullabies and very occasion-
> ally cleaned house. All this weaving, all this laundry, I
> was running out of space. And so a business was born.

She spent the early years of her career obsessively experimenting and learning about her craft. She often thought,
"Why do what a machine can do?" so she put up to eight
different yarns on the warp (such as mohair, silk, or rayon)
and contrasting weft yarns to create a blend of changing
color throughout the weave. This "color blending" approach
became her recognizable signature.

In 1978, she and her family moved to the San Francisco
Bay Area. The timing of the women's movement, which
encouraged an interest in traditional domestic crafts, lent
an atmosphere of support for her craft. She joined a
women's group that met to explore career ideas, and she
realized that she wanted to make clothing from her cloth.

Her love of clothing came to her naturally. Her father, an
immigrant Jew from Poland who ended up in Montreal,
Canada, worked his entire life as a tailor. Like the prover-
bial cobbler's daughter with no shoes, Wohl never learned
to sew as a child, but absorbed an appreciation of sewing.
After meeting a seamstress who was a part of her
women's group, she collaborated to make her first garment.

She created more clothing, and her garments got her into
her first American Craft show in 1979 where she met
Sandra Sakata, owner of an art-to-wear gallery called
Obiko in San Francisco. Through Sakata's enthusiasm and
the collaborative milieu of the early days of the art-to-wear
movement, she sold work, shared ideas, and eventually
came into her own as a designer and weaver.

After weaving cloth for almost 30 years, she is still as
enthusiastic about her medium as she was when she discovered it. For her, every piece of cloth has a narrative
quality. She never allows herself to do what she calls
"repetitive rhythmic weaving"—she must always feel
that she is making a conceptual contribution to each
part of the process:

> I love designing the warp, selecting the yarns,
> arranging the color sequences, imagining the
> weave structure. I dislike the necessary evil of
> dressing the loom…I get excited again when the
> weaving begins. The possibilities of creative explo-
> ration are not limitless, because the pattern has
> been determined and the warp colors chosen. But
> this is the aspect of weaving that is magical to me.
> Whatever yarns I choose to intersect the warp
> yarns can be predictable and original, suggest a
> road never before taken, lead me off on a new
> tangent, express an emotion, release a memory of
> a forgotten fragment of the past, stimulate an idea
> as yet unexplored.

Wohl now makes both limited production as well as
intricate one-of-a-kind pieces. All of her limited edition
weaves are variations on a theme, so each is different.
She staunchly refuses to do strict production work.
When once asked by an important client to make 50
jackets—all alike—she had to say no. "My loyalty to
the wearable movement won over my concerns for a
retirement fund," she notes with ironic humor.

GINA D'AMBROSIO
SAN ANTONIO, NEW MEXICO

"MY DESIGNS ARE TAKEN FROM THE NATU-
RALIST'S PERSPECTIVE OF THE WORLD WHICH
INCLUDES INSECTS, PLANTS, BIRDS, WATER,
OR EARTH ELEMENTS. I AM PARTICULARLY
INTERESTED IN PATTERNS DERIVED FROM
NATURE....I NOW LOOK AT LANDSAT IMAGES,
CONTOUR MAPS, FONTS AND TEXTS, ELEC-
TRON MICROSCOPIC IMAGES, MICROGRAPHS
AND THIN SECTIONS OF ROCKS AND MINER-
ALS, FOSSILS AND PALEO-PLANTLIFE, PLANK-
TONIC LIFE-FORMS FULL OF WONDERFUL
DESIGNS AND PATTERNS."

Opposite page:

**Gina D'Ambrosio, *Stratigraphica Coat*, 2001; silk and
viscose; ikat-warp-painted handwoven; discharge
printed, layered overpainting, hand printed pigment
(coat); velvet; dye-painted, hand printed
(trim and cuffs).**
Photo: Doug Merriam. Location: Sante Fe Opera;
Courtesy of Sante Fe Weaving Gallery; Sante Fe, New Mexico

Right:

**Gina D'Ambrosio, *Spirits Window Coat*, 1993; silk;
ikat-painted handwoven, mokumé-stitched resist shibori,
arashi shibori, hand printed.**

Gina D'Ambrosio conceptualizes her work from a larger perspective of ideas and techniques. A profuse experimenter and innovator of surface design on woven cloth, she been involved in textile arts in one form or another for more than 30 years.

A painter before she became involved with textiles, she also experimented with beadwork, embroidery, crochet, and knitting during the 1970s. Living in a primitive abode in New Mexico with no electricity, she raised and marketed sheep to make her living. She learned to spin and dye wool, and eventually sold the sheep in order to pursue weaving.

By 1980, she was fully involved with textiles. Painting had seemed too limiting to her, and she loved the "idea of working with shape and form" that she found in weaving. "Working in textiles has been an extension of painting for me. I am always working with color and design," she reflects.

Her painterly inclinations made it natural for her to add surface design to the handwoven cloth that she produced. In the late 1980s, she decided that she was interested in creating art-to-wear from surface-designed wovens—an idea that had been relegated mainly to wall pieces. Influenced by the work and teachings of Ana Lisa Hedstrom and Yoshika Wada, she undertook treating her woven silks with shibori and other techniques.

In 1994, her participation in a master class at Penland School of Crafts in Penland, North Carolina, taught by Jason Pollen and Joy Boutrup, had a tremendous impact on her work. This groundbreaking workshop introduced the participants to innovative textile techniques such as cloqué and devoré that weren't widely used then.

Cloqué and devoré have served as only a portion of the "palette" of techniques that she has embraced in order to give herself an endless number of choices for surface design. Add to this the possibilities of silk-screening, stamping, woodblock printing, or stenciling—and the surface vocabulary increases exponentially. "All of these processes, techniques, and layers are determined by the design idea I have for a particular cloth or for a particular collection of work," she notes, creating what she calls the "language of the cloth."

Her most recent work seems to indicate the possibility of returning to painting on canvas. She is experimenting with flat woven and surface-designed pieces whose potential functional use as a wall hanging or body shawl is secondary to its real purpose—her untiring exploration of color, line, mark, shape, and texture through the addition or subtraction of dyes to cloth. Like her surfaces, which record the memory of intricate layering and processing, her natural course of exploration continues to add a depth of field and richness to her life.

CANDISS
COLE
SEDONA, ARIZONA

"ONE OF THE MOST SATISFYING THINGS
ABOUT THE WORK THAT I DO HAPPENS
WHEN I AM IN THE DYE POTS AND DYEING
THE WARPS. I LOVE THE PROCESS OF COLOR,
THE SUBTLETY OF TONE AND HUE....IT IS
SOLITARY AND SUBJECTIVE ALL OF THE TIME."

Candiss Cole has survived and
thrived in the dual role of artist and businessperson since
1978 when she established Candiss Cole, Inc. She is the
owner/designer for the company that bears her name,
but her passion still lies in the creative, conceptual part of
her handwoven work. She relishes the process of mixing
her dyes "by eye."

Cole's garments are woven of a raw silk called silk
noil—a staple silk that is the color of a rag mop—not
considered by most to be desirable because it doesn't
have the sheen of finished silk. Nevertheless, she
prefers this material because it readily absorbs dye and
produces the saturated colors that are her hallmark.

Left:
**Candiss Cole, *Dress and Sash*, 1979;
silk/rayon warp; plain weave.**
Photo: Don Sparks

Opposite page:
**Candiss Cole, *Reflections: Swing Jacket with Matching
Vest and Scarf*, 2001; silk; handwoven, hand dyed
with ikat technique.**
Photo: John Cooper. Art director: Peter Brown

Candiss explains her dyeing and weaving process:

> Once the silk is bleached and scoured to remove all color and resists, the yarn is put into long warps that are the full length and width of the fabric. These are folded and placed in dye pots, generally moving in sections from the lightest to the darkest color. I pre-determine the size of my sections, and dye accordingly. This technique is known as ikat dyeing—a very old process used in Japan, South America, and Afghanistan, to name a few places. Once the warps are dry, they are put on the loom, to try and maintain the integrity of the color sections. Warp threading patterns and weft changes add to the textural qualities of the fabric.

All of her fabrics are woven on manual looms, and each dye lot results in a 30-yard-long bolt of fabric. Limiting the yardage and using the ikat method prevent any two garments from being exactly alike.

Her goal as a designer has been to "bridge the gap between ready-to-wear and art-to-wear," and, in this context, she considers it part of her job to respond to the needs of the consumer. Although her work is not dictated by the trends of fashion, she acknowledges that she pays attention to the changing colors of fashion. She also derives color inspiration from encounters in her daily life.

With this business-oriented outlook about her work, it is no surprise that she has spoken at conferences to her colleagues about textile and craft trends and wholesale versus retail sales. She has become a recognized leader in the crafts field in general, and the textile field in particular.

She moved to Sedona, Arizona, more than a decade ago to slow down and settle into a peaceful, contemplative environment. Instead, her career took off in a new way. She found herself on the road selling more than ever. A competent team of people now helps to run the business while she is traveling.

Above right:
Candiss Cole, *Nomadic Shawl and Mandarin Shirt*, 1999; silk; handwoven, hand dyed with ikat technique.
Photo: John Cooper
Art director: Peter Brown

Right:
Candiss Cole, *Lichen Nomadic Jacket*, 2001; silk; handwoven, hand dyed with ikat technique.
Photo: John Cooper
Art director: Peter Brown

As a child, Candiss was no stranger to the commercial side of the business that she is in today. For five generations, her family, which immigrated from Holland, worked as weavers. She grew up in and around the textile mills in Upstate New York, where members of her family wove felts for printing presses and blankets for the war effort.

When she inherited her grandparents' home, she found a treasure inside: a big box containing all of the family wool patterns brought over from Holland. Today, one of these patterns is used by Lithuanian weavers to make fabric for a collection in honor of her weaving heritage.

But Candiss never intended to become a weaver. She planned to become either a midwife or a masseuse. She went to Norway to study, but ended up at a textile school in order to learn the language before she began her training to be a midwife. By happenstance she met up with a group of Fulbright and Tiffany fellows who were traveling in Scandinavia and needed a translator. Through them she found out about the American Craft Council and its efforts to keep traditional crafts alive by providing venues for artists to sell directly to consumers. She returned to the United States in 1975 to become a part of the American Craft Movement.

Now that Cole has reached what some colleagues would consider to be a pinnacle of success with her work, she is reevaluating the focus of doing production work and the time that it takes away from learning and experimentation. During the summer of 2001 she allowed herself a precious three weeks away from her business to study at Haystack Mountain School of Crafts in Maine and Penland School of Crafts in North Carolina. As she recharges for a new period of growth in her work, it will be interesting to see where her path leads. As she thinks about the ups and downs of her career, she philosophizes: "It's easy to ride the wave—it's paddling out to meet the wave where the true test of an artist comes in."

Above left:
Candiss Cole, *Baroque Swing Jacket with Matching Vest*, 2001; silk; handwoven, hand dyed with ikat technique.
Photo: John Cooper.
Art director: Peter Brown

Left:
Candiss Cole, *Baroque Swing Jacket with Matching Vest* (back view), 2001; silk; handwoven, hand dyed with ikat technique.
Photo: John Cooper.
Art director: Peter Brown

PATRICIA PALSON

CONTOOCOOK, NEW HAMPSHIRE

"I LOVE WEAVING. IT'S A PASSION...MAYBE AN ADDICTION. I JUST KNOW I HAVE TO DO IT. WHEN I THINK ABOUT MYSELF ON A DESERTED ISLAND, I THINK I'D BE OKAY IF I HAD A LOOM. OR MAYBE I'D JUST WEAVE GRASSES....MOST DAYS I WORK FROM SEVEN IN THE MORNING TILL NINE OR TEN AT NIGHT WITH VARIOUS BREAKS LIKE WALKING WITH FRIENDS, MEALS, OR RUNNING TO THE POST OFFICE. BUT THE FACT OF THE MATTER IS THAT I LOVE MY WORK. HOW MANY PEOPLE CAN SAY THAT?"

Opposite page:
Patricia Palson, *Long Coat*, 1999; silk merino wool, rayon chenille; double ring pattern, complex twill structure.
Photo: Gina Serraino

Above:
Patricia Palson, *Jacket*, 1999; silk merino wool, rayon chenille; shimmering leaf pattern, complex twill structure.
Photo: Gina Serraino

Right:
Patricia Palson, *Jacket and Scarf*, 1999; silk merino wool, rayon chenille; shimmering leaf pattern, complex twill structure.
Photo: Gina Serraino

During the Reagan years,

when Patricia Palson quit her job as a corporate interior designer in Boston, Massachusetts, to pursue weaving, her friends thought that she had lost her mind. She and her husband were newly married without a nest egg. Yet, her husband, Eric, supported her decision, and she uncovered the loom that he had given her as a wedding present.

Weaving had been a passion for Palson long before this time. She learned to weave in college while pursuing her degree in interior design. Within a few years after her decision to work at home and weave, she gave birth to three children: Molly, Nathan, and Alex. The complexity of her new life allowed her to weave for around five to 10 minutes at a time, or—during precious nap times—about 20 minutes. She notes that weaving helped her to retain her sanity, and she wove and sold a lot of baby blankets. During 1989, between the births of Molly and Nathan, the integrity of her work led the Schacht Spindle Company to choose her to endorse their looms in weaving magazines.

An interest in eighteenth- and nineteenth-century coverlets woven in overshot patterns led her to research the patterns through two grants from the Massachusetts Arts Council. In order to reconstruct many of the patterns and put them on paper, she painstakingly counted threads by hand on coverlets that were tucked away in museum collections.

After weaving coverlets for several years, she added woven shawls to her repertoire, thinking that her customers might like wearable art. She was right. Now she uses variations of overshot patterns to create gorgeous, one-of-a-kind coats and jackets in a host of elegant designs. Working out of a

log cabin in the woods where she lives with her family, she uses computer-age technology to generate her patterns. Grateful for her life that now has more space around its events, she muses:

> There was a lot of stress in my life as an interior designer. Contractors waiting for answers. Crabby clients. This work is not life or death. Things can wait. Clients are very patient for their orders—they know I'm weaving thread by thread. It takes time.

If the obvious contentment of Patricia Palson is a result of the necessarily slow process of adding one thread at a time, perhaps her example is something to ponder in a world of rush and worry.

Opposite page:

Patricia Palson, *Jacket*, 1999; silk merino wool, rayon chenille; shimmer stripe pattern, complex twill.

Photo: Gina Serraino

Above, left:

Patricia Palson, *Coat*, 2001; silk merino wool, rayon chenille; shimmering leaf pattern, double ring pattern, shimmer stripe pattern, complex twill structure.

Photo: Jody Sinclair. Model: Molly Palson

Above, right:

Patricia Palson, *Coat*, 2001; silk merino wool, rayon chenille; shimmering leaf pattern, complex twill structure.

Photo: Jody Sinclair. Model: Molly Palson

Right:

Patricia Palson, *Jacket*, 2001; silk merino wool, rayon chenille; double ring pattern, complex twill structure.

Photo: Jody Sinclair. Model: Molly Palson

(The following information was selected for release by the artists.)

Alexis Abrams

P.O. Box 32596

Los Angeles, California 90032

Phone: (323) 221-4941

Selected galleries: Alley (Los Angeles, California), Gallery 5 (Tequesta, Florida), Gayle Willson Gallery (Southampton, New York), The Textile Museum (Washington, D.C.)

Kathryn Alexander

(in association with Carol Lee Shanks)

P.O. Box 202

Johnsonville, New York 12094

E-mail: kathalex@flash.net

Selected galleries: Julie: Artisans' Gallery (New York, New York)

Maude Andrade

P.O. Box 2728

Corrales, New Mexico 87048

Selected galleries: Bellagio (Asheville, North Carolina), Dream Weaver (Sarasota, Florida and Martha's Vineyard, Massachusetts), Julie: Artisans' Gallery (New York, New York), Rafael's (San Francisco, California), Ragazzi's Flying Shuttle (Seattle, Washington), Santa Fe Weaving Gallery (Santa Fe, New Mexico), Widney Moore Gallery (Portland, Oregon)

Selected shows: Atelier (New York, New York), Smithsonian Craft Show (Washington, D.C.)

Catherine Bacon

1682 Hill Road

Novato, California 94947

Phone: (415) 898-0770, fax: (415) 898-8889

Selected shows: Pacific Designers Collection (New York, New York)

Robin L. Bergman

(Robin Originals Creative Knits)

23 Bradford Street

Concord, Massachusetts 01742-2971

Phone: (978) 369-1925, fax: (978) 369-1925,

e-mail: robinorig@earthlink.net <www.robinoriginals.com>

Selected galleries: Bellagio (Asheville, North Carolina), J Foss, (Palo Alto, California), Maple Grove Gallery (Fish Creek, Wisconsin), Pacific Place (Seattle, Washington), Pavo Real (Boston, Massachusetts and Chicago, Illinois)

Selected shows: Atelier (New York, New York), American Craft Council (Baltimore, Maryland; San Francisco, California; St. Paul, Minnesota; Chicago, Illinois), American Craft Exposition (Evanston, Illinois), Smithsonian Craft Show (Washington, D.C.)

Selected honors, awards, exhibitions: Niche Awards (five); *Torah Cover* presented to Temple Shir Tikvah (Winchester, Massachusetts), Clothing the Muse Award, *Muse of the Millennium Invitational Fiber Exhibit*, Seattle Weavers' Guild, (Seattle, Washington), Jewish Women's Archives commission, *Ceremonial Coat* (Boston, Massachusetts)

Hulda Bridgeman

13717 N. Minihdoka

Spokane, Washington 99208

Phone: (509) 465-9591, fax: (509) 465-9591,

e-mail: hbdesign@worldnet.att.net

Selected galleries: Bellagio (Asheville, North Carolina), Dream Weaver (Sarasota, Florida and Martha's Vineyard, Massachusetts), Julie: Artisans' Gallery (New York, New York), Skera Gallery (Northampton, Massachusetts), Stowe Craft Gallery (Stowe, Vermont)

Selected shows: American Craft Council (Baltimore, Maryland), Ann Arbor Street Art Fair (Ann Arbor, Michigan), Atelier (New York, New York), Smithsonian Craft Show (Washington, D.C.)

Selected honors, awards, exhibitions: Blue Ribbon, Smithsonian Craft Show (Washington, D.C.), Niche Awards (three), Commission for permanent collection, Folklore Museum (Kwangju, South Korea)

Karren K. Brito

111 Allen

Yellow Springs, Ohio 45387

Phone: (937) 767-8961, fax: (937) 767-8961

Selected galleries: Julie: Artisans' Gallery (New York New York), Excentrique (Hinsdale, Illinois), Fabrice (Paris, France), Norma May International (Charleston, South Carolina)

Selected shows: American Craft Council (Baltimore, Maryland; Atlanta, Georgia; San Francisco, California), Atelier (New York, New York), Philadelphia Museum of Art Craft Show (Philadelphia, Pennsylvania), Smithsonian Craft Show (Washington, D.C.)

Selected honors, awards, exhibitions: Museum of Craft and Folk Art (San Francisco, California), *Materials: Hard & Soft*, Center for the Visual Arts (Denton, Texas), International Shibori Symposium, Museo de Bellas Artes (Santiago, Chile)

Jean Cacicedo

1842 San Antonio Avenue

Berkeley, California 94707

Phone: (510) 549-2251, fax: (510) 527-6401, e-mail: LCDesigns @ aol.com

Selected galleries: Julie: Artisans' Gallery (New York, New York), Santa Fe Weaving Gallery (Santa Fe, New Mexico)

Selected honors, awards, exhibitions: 30-year retrospective: *Explorations in Cloth*, Museum of Craft and Folk Art (San Francisco, California), *Made In California; Art, Image, And Identity, 1900-2000*, LA County Museum of Art (Los Angeles, California), *Celebrating American Craft*, Det Danske Kunstindustrie Museum (Copenhagen, Denmark), *Breaking Barriers: Recent American Craft*, American Craft Museum (New York, New York)

Anna Carlson

308 Prince Street, Studio 246

St. Paul, Minnesota 55101

<www.annacarlson.com>

Selected shows: American Craft Council (Baltimore, Maryland; St. Paul, Minnesota)

Nick Cave

(Nick Cave Studio)

2251 South Michigan, Suite 300

Chicago, Illinois 60616

Phone: (312) 225-2900

Selected galleries: Barbie Reed Gallery (Ketchum, Idaho), Duane Reed Gallery (St. Louis, Missouri), The Sybaris Gallery (Royal Oak, Michigan)

Selected awards, honors, exhibitions: *Body and Soul*, American Craft Museum (New York, New York), *A Typical Dress*, John Michael Kohler Arts Center (Sheboygan, Wisconsin), solo exhibition, Macalester College Art Gallery (St. Paul, Minnesota), *ZIERAT* group international exhibition (travelling the United States and Europe)

Peggotty Christensen

Selected galleries: Bellagio (Asheville, North Carolina), Dream Weaver (Sarasota, Florida; Martha's Vineyard, Massachusetts), Northern Possessions (Chicago, Illinois; Harbor Springs, Michigan), Objects (Scottsdale, Arizona; Montecito, California) Spirit of the Earth (Santa Fe, New Mexico)

Ann Clarke

463 Allen Street

Syracuse, New York 13210

Phone: (315) 478-1197, e-mail: Flaxwing@twcny.rr.com

Selected galleries: Gayle Willson Gallery

(Southampton, New York)

Candiss Cole

P.O. Box 235

Sedona, Arizona 86339

Phone: (928) 282-6490, fax: (928) 282-7948,

e-mail: candiss@candisscole.com <www.candisscole.com>

Selected galleries: Bellagio (Asheville, North Carolina), Isadora

(Sedona, Arizona), Julie: Artisans' Gallery

(New York, New York),

Rafael's (San Francisco, California) Santa Fe Weaving Gallery

(Santa Fe, New Mexico)

Selected shows: American Craft Council (Baltimore, Maryland),

Atelier (New York, New York), Sausalito Art Show (Sausalito,

California), Smithsonian Craft Show (Washington, D.C.),

Gina D'Ambrosio

P.O. Box 304

San Antonio, New Mexico 87832

Phone: (505) 835-4635, e-mail: gdambros@nmt.edu

Selected galleries: Santa Fe Weaving Gallery

(Santa Fe, New Mexico)

Randall Darwall

294 Old Main Street

Bass River, Massachusetts 02664

Phone/fax: (508) 394 6580, e-mail: MurDarOne@aol.com

Selected galleries: Bellagio (Asheville, North Carolina), Isadora

(Sedona, Arizona), Julie: Artisans' Gallery (New York, New

York), Santa Fe Weaving Gallery (Santa Fe, New Mexico),

Widney Moore Gallery (Portland, Oregon)

Selected shows: American Craft Council (Baltimore, Maryland),

American Craft Exposition (Evanston, Illinois), Philadelphia

Museum of Art Craft Show (Philadelphia, Pennsylvania),

Smithsonian Craft Show (Washington, D.C.)

*Selected awards, honors, exhibitions: Art To Wear, Poetry of

the Physical, More Than One; Men of the Cloth* (national tour),

American Craft Museum (New York, New York), award from

Boston Society of Arts and Crafts (Boston, Massachusetts)

Geneviève Dion

3249 W. Hayward Place

Denver, Colorado 80211

Phone: (303) 964-3961,

e-mail: gdion@gdion.com <www.gdion.com>

Selected galleries: Cicada (San Francisco, California), Dream

Weaver (Sarasota, Florida; Martha's Vineyard, Massachusetts),

Gayle Willson Gallery (Southampton, New York) Julie: Artisans'

Gallery (New York, New York), Rafael's (San Francisco,

California)

Selected shows: American Craft Council (Baltimore, Maryland),

Philadelphia Museum of Art Craft Show (Philadelphia,

Pennsylvania)

Selected honors, awards, exhibitions: Prize for Fiber Wearable,

Ornament magazine; U.S. National Finalist, 5th International

Textile Design Contest, Fashion Foundation of Japan; *Shibori:

Tradition and Innovations-East To West*, Museum of Craft and

Folk Art (San Francisco, California); Third International Shibori

Symposium (Santiago, Chile); *Shaped Resist: Fashion and

Textiles*, National Institute of Design, in conjunction with

Second International Shibori Symposium (Ahmedabad,

Gujarat, India)

Kay Disbrow

11 Forest Drive

Woodstock, New York 12498-1420

Phone: (845) 679-7168, fax: (845) 679-9397, e-mail:

kfiberwk@netstep.net <www. kfiberworks.com>

Selected galleries: Spirit of the Earth (Santa Fe, New Mexico),

Sweetheart Gallery (Woodstock, New York)

Selected shows: (see website listed above)

Selected honors, awards, exhibitions: inclusion in *Fiberarts

Design Book Six*, Lark Books; featured in *Ornament* magazine,

Winter 1999

Jane Dunnewold

1134 West Agarita

San Antonio, Texas 78210

Phone: (210) 733-3404, e-mail: dunnewoldj@aol.com <com-

plexcloth.com>

Selected galleries: Thirteen Moons (Santa Fe, New Mexico)

Selected shows: Houston Quilt Festival (Houston, Texas), *Quilt

National 2001*, The Dairy Barn Cultural Arts Center (Athens,

Ohio), Quilt/Surface Design Symposium

Selected honors, awards, exhibitions: Gold Prize, International

Fabric Competition (Taegu Korea); author of *Complex Cloth*

(Fiber Studio Press); past chair of Surface Design Studio,

Southwest School of Art and Craft (San Antonio, Texas)

Patricia Elmes Farley

2124 Penn Avenue, Suite 200

Pittsburgh, Pennsylvania 15222

Phone/fax: (412) 471-1930 phone/fax,

e-mail: pefar@earthlink.net <www.farleyfarley.com>

Selected galleries: Bellagio (Asheville, North Carolina),

Changes-Designs to Wear (Portland, Oregon), Gallery 5

(Tequesta, Florida), Santa Fe Weaving Gallery

(Sante Fe, New Mexico)

Selected shows: Atelier (New York, New York)

Cynthia Wayne Gaffield

24480 Orchard Lake Road

Farmington Hills, Michigan 48336

Phone: (248) 471-3873, fax: (248) 471-3898,

e-mail: textures@hotmail.com

Selected galleries: Callaway Galleries (Rochester, Minnesota),

Dream Weaver (Sarasota, Florida; Martha's Vineyard,

Massachusetts), Nubia's (Seattle, Washington), Santa Fe

Weaving Gallery (Santa Fe, New Mexico), Timna Distinctive

Artwear (Memphis, Tennessee)

Selected shows: Atelier (New York, New York), American Craft

Council (Baltimore, Maryland)

Selected honors, awards, exhibitions: included in *Fiberarts

Design Book Six* (Lark Books) and *The Complete Book of

Scarves* by J. Packham (Sterling/Chapelle)

Ellen Gienger

(EGO Originals Inc.)

EGO Art to Wear Gallery/Studio

550 S.W. Industrial Way

Bend, Oregon 97702

Phone: (541) 385-8999, e-mail: egooriginals@bendcable.com

<egooriginals.com>

Selected galleries: Bellagio (Asheville, North Carolina), Imagine

Artwear (Alexandria, Virginia), Northern Possessions (Chicago,

Illinois), Rafael's (San Francisco, California), Tempo (Newport

Beach, California)

Selected shows: American Craft Council (Baltimore, Maryland),

Pacific Designer Collection (New York, New York)

Tim Harding

(Harding Design Studio)

402 N Main Street

Stillwater, Minnesota 55082

Phone: (651)351-0383 <www.timharding.com>

Selected galleries: Bellagio (Asheville, North Carolina), Julie:

Artisans' Gallery (New York, New York), Santa Fe Weaving

Gallery (Santa Fe, New Mexico),

Widney Moore Gallery (Portland, Oregon)

Selected shows: American Craft Council (St. Paul, Minnesota),

Atelier (New York, New York), Smithsonian Craft Show

(Washington, D.C.), Philadelphia Museum of Art Craft Show

(Philadelphia, Pennsylvania)

Tim Harding (continued)

Selected honors, awards, exhibitions: work in the collections of the American Craft Museum (New York, New York), Smithsonian Museum of American Art-Renwick Gallery (Washington, D.C.), and the Minneapolis Institute of Arts (Minneapolis, Minnesota); received National Endowment for the Arts Visual Artist Fellowship; IGEDO Color Award from the Fashion Foundation of Japan

Ana Lisa Hedstrom

1420 45th Street

Emeryville, California 94608

Phone: (510) 654-4109, e-mail: hedstorms @ earthlink.net

Selected galleries: Cicada (San Francisco, California), Julie: Artisans' Gallery (New York, New York), Santa Fe Weaving Gallery (Santa Fe, New Mexico), Widney Moore Gallery (Portland, Oregon)

Selected honors, awards, exhibitions: published in *FIBERARTS* magazine (cover, 1997), *Ornament* magazine (cover photo and article, 1993), solo exhibition during 1999 at Galerie Smend (Köln, Germany), *Art, Image and Identity 1900-2000*, L.A. County Museum (Los Angeles, California); *The Kimono Inspiration*, The Textile Museum (Washington, D.C.)

Deborah Hird

1997 5th Avenue East

Kalispell, Montana 59901

Phone: (406) 755-6797, fax: (406) 755-6757, e-mail: panache@bigsky.net

Selected galleries: Bellagio (Asheville, North Carolina), Dream Weaver (Sarasota, Florida; Martha's Vineyard, Massachusetts), Imagine (Alexandria, West Virginia), Northern Possessions, (Chicago and Harbor Springs, Illinois)

Selected shows: American Craft Council (Baltimore, Maryland and San Francisco, California), Atelier (New York, New York), Smithsonian Craft Show (Washington, D.C.)

Selected awards, honors, exhibitions: Honorable Mention, Smithsonian Craft Show (Washington, D.C.); featured in *Ornament* magazine, Fall 1999; Niche Award in Fiber/Surface Design

Mary Jaeger

51 Spring Street

New York, New York 10012

Phone: (212) 941-5877, fax: (212) 625-2321, e-mail: mary@maryjaeger.com, website: www.maryjaeger.com

Selected galleries: Design in Textiles by Mary Jaeger (New York, New York), Julie: Artisans' Gallery (New York, New York)

Selected shows: Atelier (New York, New York)

Selected honors, awards, exhibitions: Association of Total Fashion, Upcoming Designer Award (Osaka, Japan); Renown Industries, New York-Tokyo Collection, Chief Designer (Tokyo, Japan); Shiho International, Shiho Collection, Chief Designer, (Kyoto, Japan and Paris, France); Distinguished Alumni Award, University of Wisconsin-Madison (Madison,Wisconsin); *Waterfalls of Rice* in Helen Allen Textile Collection, University of Wisconsin (Madison, Wisconsin)

Jorie Johnson

(Joi Rae Textiles)

1-186 Yogorocho, Momoyama, Fushimi-ku

Kyoto 612-8026 Japan

Phone/fax: 81-75-611-3800, e-mail:joirae@mb.amsinet.ne.jp <www.amsinet.ne.jp/~joirae>

Selected galleries: Design in Textiles by Mary Jaeger (New York, New York), Gallery Gallery (Kyoto, Japan), Wacoal Ginza Art Space (Ginza, Tokyo)

Selected awards, honors, exhibitions: Japan Creations, Japan Textile Designer's Association Award; First Prize, Virtuoso Fabrics Exhibition, HGA Convergence

Mike Kane and Steve Sells

(Kane & Sells Studio)

Phone/fax: (828) 765-8492, e-mail:theboys@m-y.net

Selected galleries: Bellagio (Asheville, North Carolina), Dream Weaver (Sarasota, Florida), Northern Possessions (Chicago, Illinois), Skera Gallery (Northampton, Massachusetts)

Selected shows: American Craft Council shows, Atelier (New York, New York), Philadelphia Museum of Art Craft Show (Philadelphia, Pennsylvania), Smithsonian Craft Show (Washington, D.C.)

Renita G. Kuhn

(in association with Jane Dunnewold)

8628 Stone Harbor Avenue

Las Vegas, Nevada 89145

Phone: (702) 256-5876, fax: (702) 256-9603

Selected galleries: Textures Gallery (San Antonio, Texas), Ursaline Gallery (San Antonio, Texas)

Michelle Marcuse

1400 North 4th Stree

Philadelphia, Pennsylvania 19122

Phone: (215) 235-3483, fax: (215) 236-3041, e-mail: michellemarcuse@aol.com <www.inliquid.com>

Selected galleries: Arte (Cincinatti, Ohio), Gayle Willson Gallery (Southampton, New York), smARTwear (Carmel-by-the-Sea, California)

Selected shows: Atelier (New York, New York), The Philadelphia Museum of Art Craft Show (Philadelphia, Pennsylvania), Smithsonian Craft Show, Washington, D.C.

Selected honors, awards, exhibitions: The 2nd Taegu International Textile Design Competition (Taegu, Korea); *African Presence—Visual Activism in Philadelphia*, African American Museum (Philadelphia, Pennsylvania); Honorable Mention in Fiber Arts, The Leeway Foundation (Philadelphia, Pennsylvania); *Cultural Fiber*, The Bangkok Collection, United States Embassy, (Bangkok, Thailand)

Ellen Marsh and Robin McKay

Robin McKay (Studio E)

84 Walker Street

New York, New York 10013

Phone: (212) 219-1837; e-mail-robinmckay@earthlink.net

Ellen Marsh (Studio E)

2969 Fairoaks Avenue

Redwood City, California 94063

Phone: (650) 367-7880-e-mail: ellenjylmarsh@earthlink.net

Selected shows: Pacific Designer Collection (New York, New York)

Selected honors, awards, exhibitions: Fusion Artwear, Oakland Museum (Oakland, California); *To the Beat of Africa*, The Craft and Folk Art Museum (San Francisco, California); *Art To Wear*, Palo Alto Art Center, (Paolo Alto, California); *International Photography Exhibit of Shibori Artists,* The American Chilean Institute (Santiago, Chile)

Joan McGee

8246 Coash Road

Sarasota, Florida 34241

Phone: (941) 926-0465, fax: (941) 926-0466, e-mail: mcgeejoan @ aol.com

Selected galleries: Bellagio (Asheville, North Carolina), Isadora (Sedona, Arizona), Julie: Artisans' Gallery (New York, New York), Northern Possessions (Chicago, Illinois), Rafaels (San Francisco, California)

Selected shows: Pacific Designer Collection (New York, New York), Smithsonian Craft Show (Washington, D.C.)

Michelle Murray

P.O. Box 1437

St. Augustine, Florida 32085

E-mail: mmm@aug.com

Selected galleries: Bellagio (Asheville, North Carolina), Julie: Artisans' Gallery (New York, New York), Ragazzi's Flying Shuttle (Seattle, Washington), Studio 40, Greenbrier Hotel (White Sulphur Springs, West Virginia), Widney Moore Gallery

(Portland, Oregon)

Selected shows: American Craft Council (Baltimore, Maryland), Philadelphia Museum of Art Craft Show (Philadelphia, Pennsylvania), Smithsonian Craft Show (Washington D.C.)

Patricia Palson
1111 Pine Street
Contoocook, New Hampshire 03229
Phone: (603) 746-6558, e-mail: ppalson@aol.com
Selected galleries: Northern Possessions (Chicago, Illinois), Changes (Portland, Oregon), Dream Weaver (Sarasota, Florida), The Textile Museum (Washington D.C.), The Yarrow Collection (Santa Fe, New Mexico)
Selected shows: American Craft Council (Baltimore, Maryland), Crafts at the Castle (Boston, Massachusetts), Paradise City (Northhampton, New York), League of New Hampshire Craftsmen (Sunapee, New Hampshire)
Selected honors, awards, exhibitions: Weaver of Distinction, New England Weavers Seminar; Best of Show, League of New Hampshire Craftsmen (Sunapee, New Hampshire)

Sally Ryan
10548 Winston Lane
Fishers, Indiana 46038
Phone: (317) 845-3440, fax: (317) 845-3440, e-mail: salryan@home.com <www.sallyryan.com>
Selected galleries: Bellagio (Asheville, North Carolina), Changes-Designs to Wear (Portland, Oregon), Imagine Artwear (Alexandria, Virginia), W.O.W.-Wonderful Ornament for Women (Newton Highlands, Massachusetts)
Selected shows: American Craft Council Craft (Baltimore, Maryland; Chicago, Illinois; and San Francisco, California), Philadelphia Museum of Art Craft Show (Philadelphia, Pennsylvania), Crafts at the Castle (Boston, Massachusetts)
Selected awards, honors, exhibitions: Niche Awards (three), Ohio Designer Craftsmen Award for Excellence (two)

Laurie Schafer
1133 Harwich Drive
San Marcos, California 92069
Phone: (651) 503-0474 or(760) 744-8963,
fax: (760) 744-8623, e-mail: bodygeometry@earthlink.net <www.laurieschafer.com>
Selected galleries: Bellagio (Asheville, North Carolina), Cicada (San Francisco, California), Gallery 5 (Tequesta, Florida), Kittie Kyle (Memphis, Tennessee), La Jolla Fiber Arts (La Jolla, California)
Selected shows: American Craft Council (St. Paul, Minnesota), Artwear in Motion (Minneapolis, Minnesota), Artwear

(Fort Collins, Colorado), Atelier (New York, New York)
Selected honors, awards, exhibitions: work in the collection of Goldstein Gallery, University of Minnesota, and the Minnesota Historical Society; Minnesota Artist Award, American Craft Council; Juror's Award, Artwear (Fort Collins, Colorado); featured in *Ornament* magazine's Twentieth Anniversary Issue

Carol Lee Shanks
3102 Wheeler Street
Berkeley, California 94705-1829
Phone: (510) 548-5979, fax: (510) 548-5979, e-mail: clshanks@earthlink.net
Selected galleries: Julie Artisans' Gallery (New York, New York)
Selected honors, awards, exhibitions: *Shibori: Tradition and Innovation-East to West*, Museum of Craft and Folk Art (San Francisco, California)

Carter Smith
25 Pleasant Street
Nahant, Massachusetts 01908
Phone: (781) 581-9706, fax: (781) 581 3267, e-mail: carter@shibori.com <shibori.com>
Selected galleries: Julie: Artisans' Gallery (New York, New York), Kapsiki (Palm Beach, Florida), Northern Possessions (Chicago, Illinois), Valentina (Brookfield, Wisconsin)
Selected shows: Designers at the Essex House (New York, New York)
Selected awards, honors, or exhibitions: *The Kimono Influence*, Textile Museum (Washington, D.C.); *Shibori*, Museum of Craft and Folk Art (San Francisco, California); *Shibori Unbound*, Cincinnati Contemporary Art Center (Cincinnati, Ohio)

Jane Steinsnyder
(Cassowary)
621 Reed Street
Philadelphia, Pennsylvania 19147
Phone: (215) 551-9955, fax: (215) 551-9955, e-mail: cassowar@earthlink.net
Selected galleries: Cicada (San Francisco, California), Excentrique, (Hinsdale, Illinois), Fibers and Fantasy (Ithaca, New York), Origins (Santa Fe, New Mexico), Touches (Philadelphia, Pennsylvania)
Selected shows: American Craft Council (Baltimore, Maryland), Atelier (New York, New York), Philadelphia Museum of Art Craft Show (Philadelphia, Pennsylvania)

Susan Summa
210 East Houghton Street
Santa Fe, New Mexico 87505
Phone: (505) 982-9112, fax: (505) 982-5909, e-mail: chinasue@earthlink.net
Selected galleries: Santa Fe Weaving Gallery (Santa Fe, New Mexico)
Selected shows: Atelier (New York, New York)

Mark Thomas
Phone: (415) 864-4746, fax: (415) 864-4746, e-mail: mttextile@aol.com
Selected galleries: Bellagio (Asheville, North Carolina), Dream Weaver (Sarasota, Florida; Martha's Vineyard, Massachusetts), Janet Foss (Palo Alto, California), Northern Possessions (Chicago, Illinois; Harbor Springs, Michigan), Spirit of the Earth (Santa Fe, New Mexico)
Selected shows: American Craft Council (Baltimore, Maryland), Sausalito Arts Festival (Sausalito, California), Smithsonian Craft Show (Washington, D.C.)
Selected honors, awards, exhibitions: First Place, Mill Valley Arts Festival (California); Second Place, Sausalito Arts Festival (Sausalito, California)

Arlene Wohl
244 Glen Drive
Sausalito, California 94965
Phone: (415) 332-5216, fax: (415) 332-0821,
e-mail: arlwohl@aol.com
Selected galleries: Dream Weaver (Sarasota, Florida; Martha's Vineyard, Massachusetts), Julie: Artisans' Gallery (New York, New York), Mio (San Francisco, California), Ragazzi's Flying Shuttle (Seattle, Washington)
Selected shows: American Craft Council (San Francisco, California; Baltimore, Maryland), Atelier (New York, New York), Philadelphia Museum of Art Craft Show (Philadelphia, Pennsylvania), Sausalito Arts Festival (Sausalito, California), Smithsonian Craft Show (Washington, D.C.)
Selected honors, awards, exhibitions: Best of Show, Sausalito Arts Festival (Sausalito, California), Philadelphia Museum of Art Craft Show (Philadelphia, Pennsylvania), Excellence Award, Baltimore Craft Show (Baltimore, Maryland)

Appliqué. A cutout design element, such as a piece of fabric, that is attached to the surface of fabric through sewing or other means.

Batik. Textile craft, originating from Java, which consists in drawing a design on cloth with liquid wax and immersing the fabric in dyes which resist the waxed areas. After the wax is melted, the drawn pattern is left visible in the original ground color. This process is repeated for each color.

Blockprinting. Hand process which allows images to be stamped on cloth with the use of incised wooden or metal blocks.

Cloqué. A technique in which portions of fabric are shrunk by chemical shrinking agents, causing the unaffected fabric to pucker in a controlled way. (This technique originated in the textile industry where it was used to produce seersucker.)

Couture. The business of designing, making, and selling fashionable custom-made clothing; also, the designers and establishments engaged in the business.

Dextrin resist. A vegetable paste made of potato (dextrin) powder that is spread on selected areas of fabric to create surface designs before being allowed to dry and crackle. Dyes are then spread over the resist to penetrate the cracks. The dextrin is eventually removed to reveal the pattern.

Devoré. A technique which uses a chemical to burn out, or remove, areas of bast fibers in a textile. After the burn out, man-made fibers, protein fibers, or plant fibers protected by a resist will remain, unaffected.

Loom. Apparatus for weaving cloth made by interlacing yarns at right angles; the warp being under tension, and the weft threaded through.

Shibori. A technique of manipulating and shaping cloth before dyeing it, so that it takes the dye in blurry-edged patterns. Shiboru, the Japanese root word, means to wring, squeeze, or press. Shibori methods include folding, stitching, crumpling, twisting, plucking, and plaiting. Many contemporary art-to-wear artists clamp the fabric between boards or wrap the fabric around plastic plumbing pipe as a part of this process. The cloth is then secured in various ways such as knotting or binding it. The variables of shaping the cloth coupled with the unpredictable nature of the dye pot, lend some unpredictable results to the processs.

Silk-screening. A form of stenciling on silk, carried out by hand. The design requires a separate screen for each color, and various methods can be used to apply the design.

Warp and weft. Warp threads are spaced and set on the loom running the length of a piece of woven cloth. A selvedge or strengthened border is made at each side. The intersecting threads which weave the cloth are known as the weft; these cross the warp at right angles running from selvedge to selvedge.